MAN OF INFLUENCE

FOLLOWING THE MASTER, LEAVING A LEGACY

JIM COTÉ

InterVarsity Press
Downers Grove, Illinois

InterVarsity Press
P.O. Box 1400, Downers Grove, IL 60515-1426
World Wide Web: www.ivpress.com
E-mail: mail@ivpress.com

InterVarsity Press® is the book-publishing division of InterVarsity Christian Fellowship/USA®, a student movement active on campus at hundreds of universities, colleges and schools of nursing in the United States of America, and a member movement of the International Fellowship of Evangelical Students. For information about local and regional activities, write Public Relations Dept., InterVarsity Christian Fellowship/USA, 6400 Schroeder Rd., P.O. Box 7895, Madison, WI 53707-7895.

Cover photograph: Paul Chesley/Stone

ISBN 0-8308-2298-4

Printed in the United States of America ∞

Library of Congress Cataloging-in-Publication Data

Coté, Jim
    Man of influence : following the Master, leaving a legacy / Jim Coté.
        p. cm.
    Includes bibliographical references.
    ISBN 0-8308-2298-4 (alk. paper)
     1. Jesus Christ—Example. 2. Christian life. I. Title.
    BT304.2 .C66 2001
    232.9'04—dc21

                                                                                                2001024042

25 24 23 22 21 20 19 18 17 16 15 14 13 12 11 10 9 8 7 6 5 4 3 2 1

22 21 20 19 18 17 16 15 14 13 12 11 10 09 08 07 06 05 04 03 02 01

Surely this book is dedicated to God, my Savior,
Lord and friend, that he might use it to accomplish his purposes and bring
honor to himself—that would be an incredible outcome of this publication!

Also, this book needs to be dedicated to all the men who have influenced
my life in the past—my dad, my coaches, my pastors and my mentors,
as well as my friends. Furthermore, this book is dedicated to the current
audience of men who will read the contents, that together we will
become the Master's men—one and all.

Finally, this book is dedicated to my three sons,
who represent the future—Matthew, Daniel and Nathan.
They have taught me the significance of needing to be a responsible male,
and now I pray they will continue to develop as men of God
and as such stand firm in the Lord.

CONTENTS

Acknowledgments

I thank God for the privilege of writing and the honor of trying to communicate his truth to my generation. I want to express my appreciation to the wonderful folk at InterVarsity Press, especially Jeff Crosby and Andy Le Peau, who were able not only to catch the vision of this manuscript but to bring it to completion.

Finally, and most important, I want to thank my beautiful wife of twenty-five years, Brenda, who not only encouraged me to complete the manuscript but helped type it and has enjoyed the process with me each step of the way.

Introduction

Ever wonder whether you made the right investment decision with your life? As I reviewed the paper this afternoon, I found myself wondering about the best definition of *net worth*. In recent years we have seen the stock market reaching record highs, athletes negotiating bigger and richer contracts, and the economy making most people's wallets fatter—both here and in the emerging markets in Asia. But what about less tangible investments? How does someone who has invested heavily in human need and development calculate whether their less tangible efforts are creating value and paying dividends? In other words, can the value of a life be measured any other way than numerically and esteemed for values that aren't merely economic?

For years now, economic expansion and the technology, people, marketing programs and interest rates that have propelled us there have dominated the headlines. And today's heroes, ultimately, have been those leading the parade of financial advancement that marked the last decade of the last century of the past millennium.

So, is a decision to invest in people wrong or naive, especially if it conflicts with an opportunity to advance materially? Today as the world strives to accelerate financially, the question that stirs within me is this: What is the supreme opportunity of life? What value surpasses all others so that the pursuit of it guarantees the satisfaction of a life well spent and without regrets?

As I read the headlines about today's successful people and reflect on this great question of purpose, production and quality, my mind flashes back to another person of another era who died broke, though he was one of the most respected personalities of the twentieth century.

Alvin York, an American hero in World War I, with unlimited potential to increase his income from the marketing of his military exploits, died nearly penniless. It was not because he squandered his wealth but because he gave it away, defining wealth by the number of people he could help and not by financial accumulation made possible by a moment of incredible success. York refused to sell his uniform and profit from the results of God's providential protection of his life during the war. He felt that cashing in on his war exploits, when so many American soldiers died doing what he did—his duty—was tantamount to grave robbing. York never considered himself a hero,[1] only an obedient soldier, so he elected to maintain a perspective that viewed helping the helpless without selling his soul to Madison Avenue as a higher calling and nobler enterprise. Knowing his own propensity to err and recognizing the incomparable temptation that fame and fortune would bring him, York purposely refused lucrative movie, book and endorsement deals in order to focus on founding an educational institute for the rural poor and uneducated children of his home state of Tennessee. Alvin York spent a lifetime raising money to fund his nonprofit institute. He rarely took a salary and died without the comforts of material success. Yet at his funeral the nation stopped to mourn. Over eight thousand people paid tribute at the gravesite, including the governor of Tennessee and other dignitaries.

So was his life successful? Was it well spent? By what calculation do we measure the worth of a life? I suppose by the values that such a life reflects and extends forward. These values for York were honesty, diligence, compassion and personal care for those who were helpless and hopeless.

But what of today's values? How do we measure the success of a life being well lived? Recently computer giant Microsoft was found by a federal judge to be a monopolistic enterprise that squelches the innovation and opportunities of its competitors, harming both them and the consumers who purchase their products. And what was Wall Street's reaction to such a dastardly deed? Nearly nothing. Microsoft shrugged off the bad news, hardly dropping in value before it headed back up in price for its investors. Why? Don't we care about integrity, fair play and honest competition? Or have we sacrificed such fundamental virtues for the more glamorous results of a fattened stock portfolio and the material benefits it affords us? Are there any Alvin Yorks today?

What is the value of life? What purpose should I live for? What results do I want to achieve? How can I invest my years so that ultimately I am satisfied with the effort, process, progress and outcomes? How can I, when all is said and done, guarantee that I can look back with confidence that I have lived without regret? In a phrase, it's up to me. And you—how do you want to be remembered? What legacy do you want to leave? What residual effect can you take with you? How can you be a man of influence?

For me, the answer is people. The best enterprise for me is one that considers what's best for others. That endeavor needs to be a steady, constructive effort to apply my gifts, experience, resources and relationships to help others to do their best. If I can lift the life experience of other people higher than it would have been without me, then my life has counted for something greater than just lifting myself. Whether I am engaged in a for-profit or nonprofit enterprise, if what I do contributes to the life health of others in a meaningful and lasting way, then I have succeeded in leveraging my life multiple times by all those I've helped. That's a good investment. And if what I do helps others to replicate that altruistic effort, then my leverage is multiplied further. In the process, no doubt, my needs will be met—but better yet, when my life's sun begins to set, I will have the satisfaction of knowing I'm leaving behind a better world, a host of appreciative friends and a legacy that shall endure beyond me, my 401(k) plan and my fishing boat.

Most of the men I meet want something similar. Ask a guy when he's alone and serious what he wants to do with his life, and he'll undoubtedly say, "I want to make a difference." Even the young men I meet, who have yet to learn that achievement and accumulation don't ultimately satisfy, will say they want to make their money, see their world and rule from the top so they can help others. So how is it that so many have gotten off track? Why is it that the young man's idealism gets misdirected toward self-advancement, acquisition and accomplishment? And how is it that most middle-aged men are still looking for a place to plant their hearts in order to use their remaining years, gifts and energies for something bigger than themselves?

I believe that it is because most men are missing a hero, someone who models their highest ideals and inspires them to strive valiantly to achieve them. We men are looking for another man who demonstrates the particulars of a noble lifestyle in the grit and grime of a normal, daily existence. We don't really have a teaching model to follow. Few are successful enough to engender our confidence, create courage and inspire perseverance to tough it out through the difficult attempt to live cross-grained to the culture and our human nature. After all, many leaders today are as lost as their followers.

If you are with me so far, don't despair; I think I've found a hero you'll like.

First I need to tell you that something strange has happened to me in the last twenty years. I've begun to love people. I didn't always, but I learned to love them from someone who personifies love. His name is Jesus Christ. His life account is recorded in a book known as the Bible. His life pattern was similar to the one I described earlier—Sergeant York's. But Christ's life was superior. He perfectly personified a "without regret" investor by living a life committed to being there for others, caring for them, teaching them and helping them to a higher place spiritually, emotionally, physically and relationally. He died penniless—but not forgotten. And his life literally changed the world.

Consider the perfect example of this selfless man. Nearly two thousand years after his death, he is still the most revered person of history. We mark our calendars by his birth and internationally celebrate it as a holiday. Yet for all he did and died for, one of his most remarkable, practical accomplishments was that he taught men and women how to treat one another with dignity and respect, which resulted in a transformed community and later a transformed society. No one who knew him intimately went without being deeply affected by him, and his followers most willingly replicated his life pattern by dedicating their lives to helping others find a better life.

And this same process of moral imitation is taking place today, generations after his generation. I suppose that proves the point that he invested his life well, for the compounding effect of his life philosophy and behavior is still gaining momentum after two thousand years. And I think that is because when you really get to know him, you'll find him so relatable and inspiring.

That's the philosophy I want to copy. His life is the one I want to emulate. I am not ready to die or be broke, nor am I advocating such a radical sacrifice. But I do want to make a significant, lasting difference in the lives of others, and I do want to be remembered for what I gave, not what I got. I want to leave a legacy. I want to be a man who influenced others in a lasting way.

As I compare the option of unmitigated financial advancement solely for the sake of my own indulgence against the option of using my resources to advance the quality of life of those in need, I vote for option two.

So a life invested in doing the right thing for the right reasons is not a life wasted—only tested. Anyone who has made a decision to live nobly has made the right decision, even if it hasn't earned him a fortune. Happier still is the thought that from this day forward we can spend our lives on something more significant than personal success. We can still leverage our life for good.

I've learned a lot from this master of influence named Jesus. I have also had the privilege in the last twenty-five years of teaching others what he has been teaching me. I want to continue to be a student and a practitioner for there is so much to learn and do. I am going to move forward, in fact, to review ten principles of successful life investing as modeled by the Master. Why don't you join me on this educational tour, and let's see if, at the end, we are not better people for it and able to help our world be a little better as well.

Here we go . . .

1

REALLY GETTING STARTED

*E*veryone marks his or her life by that of Jesus Christ—even if it's unwittingly. I once heard a journalist on National Public Radio report on a find of ancient artifacts in China. When she described their age, she dated them from the time of Christ. How ironic. Even an *impartial*, secular journalist needed to refer to the world's most renowned religious figure in order to report the news accurately. So, in fact, do we all. Our calendars and even the date we write at the top of our checks reckon time from the birth of Christ. That same week of the news story I visited one of the state parks near my home in North Carolina. To my amusement, when I asked the park ranger what days the park was accessible, he stated that it was open every day of the year except Christmas. How about that? The government famous for its inverse protection of the "wall of separation between church and state" nevertheless takes off the founder of the church's birthday as its only national holiday. No matter how hard a person might try to deny the incredible impact of the life of the carpenter from Nazareth, he or she is bound to run up against the fact that the influence of Jesus Christ continues to be felt today. His footprints seem to be everywhere, from the orientation of our calendars to the content of our moral codes, to the popular phrases we use such as "do unto others" and "seek and you shall find," or that famous quote mistakenly attributed to Abraham Lincoln: a "household divided against itself will not stand" (Matthew 12:25).

This soliloquy titled "One Solitary Life" says it best:

> He was born in an obscure village, the child of a peasant woman. He grew up in still another village, where he worked in a carpenter's shop until he was thirty. Then for three years he was an itinerant preacher. He never wrote a book. He never held an office. He never had a family or owned a house. He did not go to college. He never visited a big city. He did none of the things one usually associates with greatness. He had no credentials but himself. He was only thirty-three when the tide of public opinion turned against him. His friends ran away. He was turned over to his enemies and went through the mockery of a trial. He was nailed to a cross between two thieves. While he was dying, his executioners gambled for his clothing, the only property he had on earth. When he was dead, he was laid in a borrowed grave through the pity of a friend. Nineteen centuries have come and gone, and today he remains the central figure of the human race, and the leader of mankind's progress. All the armies that ever sailed, all parliaments that ever sat, all the kings that ever reigned, put together, have not affected the life of man on this planet so much as that one solitary life.[1]

So if these statements are true, if he is the most influential person of human history, then my curiosity prompts the question, "How did he do it?" By what power or plan was he able to accomplish a life of such significance? And if I discover those plans, can I employ the same methods to guarantee that my life will impact the world with such force as to arrest the attention of a future generation?

The answer, I have discovered in reverse order, is yes. My life lived Jesus' way can be influential into succeeding generations. Also, his life indeed had a method to it that was purposeful, discernible and replicable. His enabling came from a higher power that allowed him to rise above the mediocrity of common society to a place of unparalleled effectiveness and efficiency.

Sure, he is God's Son and I am not, but his human characteristics can be imitated, and, better yet, he discloses that the power that enabled him is available to us as well. The only condition for those who are curious is the simple invitation once given to a man named Nathanael: "Come and see" (John 1:46).

So we have an uncommon opportunity with uncommon implications. We are given a chance to check him out and learn from his example. If we do, we then have his promise to empower us in such a way that our lives will actually begin to reflect his in quality, influence and outcome.[2] Let's take him up on his offer. Let's look directly into his life experiences from a chronological, historical record authored by a physician named Luke. This account will enable us to see how he got started, what he did, how he did it, whom he was associated with and what resulted.

We will begin our review of this significant life by pulling the curtain back on the stage to see Jesus' induction into his life's work. Jesus was a traveling lecturer with a message of spiritual emancipation. His vocational story begins on the banks of the Jordan River, in the country of Palestine, during a baptismal service conducted by a local revivalist known as John the Baptist. This account, in the book of Luke in the New Testament, is acknowledged for its accuracy and completeness. We pick up the story in the third chapter.

In verse 3 we read something of the message of the revivalist John that reveals the theme and significance of the ministry of Jesus: "He [John] went into all the country around the Jordan, preaching a baptism of repentance for the forgiveness of sins."

Those few words tell us a lot about the spiritual climate of this event. Apparently there was widespread indifference to the destructive nature of wrongdoing (sin). Ignorance of the fact that the Creator was disappointed with the population and demanding a change of heart is what prompted John to preach.

Of course, changed behavior (repentance) can only be sustained if there is first a changed heart. And the evidence of a changed heart in this first-century Jewish society was the religious ritual of baptism (ceremonial washing). People do not jump into a cold river with all their clothes on unless they are convinced that the effort holds some importance for their lives. So baptism was one of the signature religious rituals that Israel used in order to document a changed condition in the life of a believer in God.

Many people, we read, came to John that day needing this cleansing event. But the most noticeable person to step into the water was Jesus. He was the long-awaited Messiah of Israel, the one they looked to be a savior, deliverer and king of the people of God (Micah 5:2-5).

John was forewarned of Jesus' arrival by a dream, and yet John deferred to Jesus when Jesus asked to be baptized.[3] John knew Jesus was in no need of the cleansing ritual, for Christ's heart and life were perfect, without sin. But Jesus wanted to submit to the sacred ordinance of the Mosaic law (Israel's religious code) as a model for others. So on Jesus' insistence, John baptized him. However, what happened next was both unusual and never duplicated. Luke writes that, first, heaven opened and a dove (representative of the Spirit of God) landed on Jesus. Second, the voice of God boomed from above them with the acclamation that this Jesus was his Son (rightful heir to God's throne) and that he, the heavenly Father, was well satisfied with the relationship, role and reputation of his Son.

This was extremely unusual. But so what? What does this have to do with me? Everything, if you want to live a life of influence, with significance and without regret. This event represents an event we too must go through if we are to be accepted into the fraternity of Christ—what some call being a Christian.

Unlike Jesus, we have plenty of blemishes on our lives. And all these blemishes (behavioral wrongdoing) begin with a blemish on the heart—our moral generator. If your moral generator is right, you'll do right, but if it's not, you can't help but err. You're only human; it's only natural. In fact, the Bible recognizes the universal fact of sin[4] and even provides us with the answer to why we sin.[5]

But the main point is this: we need a cleansed heart—we need a bath—we need spiritual baptism if we are to have a healthy moral generator. John the Baptist symbolized this internal, invisible activity by dunking people in a river. And the issue remains the same today. With or without water we all need a clean heart, and that only comes from God. He alone has the power to forgive and the right to do so, since the penalty for our mistakes has been paid by someone else, whose name is Jesus.

I guess I am getting ahead of myself, but let me say it here. Jesus Christ, God's Son, came to earth for expressly that purpose—to pay the penalty of our sins. Sin is a debt to our Creator, who is without sin. It's against his nature, and it evokes his displeasure. In fact, as promised[6] and repeated in Scripture,[7] sin's penalty is death.

So Jesus, sinless and guiltless, paid that price for all when he was punished by God, the Father, while hanging on a Roman crucifixion timber in A.D. 34. He rose from the dead three days later by the power of the same life-giving Spirit that landed on his shoulder the day of his baptism.[8] And he now promises that same life-giving Spirit and life-enabling power to all who will believe he died specifically for them.[9]

When we do believe, we receive all the blessings and benefits that God originally intended for the human race.[10] Of course, Jesus, never having sinned, never lost the blessings and benefits of perfect communion with the heavenly Father, which explains why the same Father would shout from the heavens how proud he was of his Son. That brings us to you and me. Those same three events need to be a part of our life experience before we embark on a journey with the Master. For Jesus is not really our master if we've rejected his offer of forgiveness of sins and a new heart. Also, we will never have the power to follow and imitate him if we are not made of the same spiritual stuff.

If we don't have his Spirit in our heart, then we don't stand a chance of becoming a Master's man. We can try, but we will fail miserably because we first need to be transformed spiritually by the new birth (new heart), which is derived from being a believer in Jesus Christ. There is no other way.

This prospect may sound odd at first, but perhaps this story will illustrate how contemporary and relevant it really is.

About twenty-five years ago a young man, just eighteen, held up a 7-Eleven store in central Louisiana. He was caught and jailed, and a trial date was set. His mother, however, had other ideas. She was a desperate woman, and her story was a sad one, which she used to appeal to the trial judge. She begged him to grant clemency to her son. It seems that her boy was the oldest of eight children, the youngest being but a few months old.

Apparently the stress and strain of supporting such a large family had gotten the worst of the father, so he left, leaving this mom with sole responsibility of supporting herself and the children. Life was hard. She took in wash to earn money and her eighteen-year-old worked at a service station in order to help her pay the bills. They were too proud for welfare and too limited vocationally to break out of the cycle of poverty.

Then the worst happened. The baby became ill and needed medical attention. Not having any money for doctors or medicine, the older son panicked, took his father's hunting rifle and held up a convenience store. So now the mom's only option, it seemed, was to implore the good judge, someone with whom she had gone to high school, to let her son go. "The boy had no previous arrest record—not even a traffic violation. He had made a stupid mistake," she reasoned. "No one was hurt, and he did it for the right reasons."

She heard back promptly from the judge. He knew the family and understood. In fact, her son had serviced his automobile several times. But the judge explained that he was bound by the laws and jurisdiction of the state of Louisiana and sworn to uphold them. He assured her of a fair trial but also reminded her that the boy would have to pay for his crime (error) as the law pronounced.

The trial date came, and the boy was found guilty. Since it was a first-time offense, he could get a probated sentence, but he would have to pay a fine of $2,500—an immense amount by the family's standards—or he was off to prison for at least six years. The gavel fell, the boy was declared guilty.

But then the judge did a remarkable thing. He stood from his chair, took off his robe, walked down to the bailiff, pulled out his checkbook and told the bailiff he would pay the boy's fine. And pay it he did—he wrote a personal check for $2,500, and the boy went free.

Incredible. How generous. How merciful. And brilliant, for the law's demands were also met, without injury to a repentant party. That is exactly what Jesus did for you and me.

The heavenly Father, who is holy and has his rules of conduct that demand retribution if broken, is just like that judge. He too must uphold the jurisdiction of his position or, theoretically, forfeit it. So what is he to do? The penalty of sin, according to God's law, is physical and spiritual death, which biblically means *separation*. We have all broken this law, and we all sense this separation. But because of his love and generosity, God paid our fine through the person of his Son, who died in our place that fateful Friday in A.D. 34. As a result, we go free—if we accept his payment.

It's so easy that most people miss it. It's so profound that I am still struck by its wonder, though it has been thirty years since I accepted Christ's payment.

To repeat:

1. We all need to recognize our errors and repent—turn from wrong toward God.

2. We all need to be cleansed by trusting Christ's death—a payment for our sins.[11]

3. When we do, we receive the presence and power of God's Spirit in us, enabling us to live for God and please him—just as Jesus did.

What an incredible offer. What a life-changing opportunity. If you have not been initiated into Christianity yet, why not do it now by simply telling God you believe and receive him in application of those three prescriptions listed above? The rest of your life awaits your decision.

2

TEMPTATION

Trial Before Triumph

LUKE 4:1-13

*I*n 1999, for the first time in United States history, an elected president was impeached on perjury and obstruction of justice charges. Just before that, two Republican Speakers of the House resigned in response to accusations of marital infidelity. The president did not resign, however, but served out his full term after being acquitted by the Senate.

What was originally at issue was the president's morality, or better, his definition of morality. The majority of the members of the House of Representatives found William Jefferson Clinton's dalliances, sexual indiscretions and professional irresponsibility in the discharge of his duties so egregious that they voted for the president's legal removal from office. They wondered out loud whether his judgment was so impaired by his prurient interests as to diminish his ability to lead. His sexual escapades were seen as a threat to the competent functioning of his duties as the chief executive officer of the government of the United States. Therefore, his colleagues felt compelled to bring charges against him, convinced that he had lost the wisdom and privilege to lead.

And the result? Nothing happened.

Just a year later no one even talked of it anymore. The sordid affair was passé. Mr. Clinton remained in office, and it seems that the public backlash at the House of Representatives' attempt to uphold the Constitution as well as the integrity of the chief executive's office was found by the voting public to be unwarranted. Tuned to the ever-changing winds of public opinion, the Senate accurately assessed the consensus of the people's attitude and voted down the article to impeach by an impressive margin. And so our nation's chief executive, despite his hubris, remained in office to govern, establish policy, pass executive orders and appoint key federal and judicial officials just as before. "Only in America," they say.

Besides what this says about the American public's perspective on their presidents' virtues such as chastity, fidelity, self-control and self-sacrifice, it causes me to ponder what this says about our new expectations of the qualifications of those who seek to govern us. What is the new definition of a leader? If not honor, nobility and prudence, as well as kindness, compassion and generosity, then what? Perhaps the new definition is nimble-footedness in the face of judicial inquiries and the ability to compartmentalize personal and public lives.

I want to know what virtues, when displayed by those who govern, provide inspiration, guidance and hope to folk who follow and who would otherwise lose their way.

Or perhaps the question must first be asked and answered, "What's the goal we're aiming at that defines the ultimate credibility of a national leader?" If we can discover that one target that epitomizes the attributes of personal character qualifying one for true leadership, then surely any sacrifice given, any effort expended, any time invested toward the achievement of that goal would be applauded as the rightful use of a life. And it naturally follows that the absence of those pursuits would be recognized as a disqualifier.

So what is a model worth replicating? Is there a personality whose quality of life inspires the generations that follow to live in such a way that the result is the elevation of society? Who then can we follow? Who would more closely reflect the standard of noble virtue and inspiring character that would stimulate uncompromised allegiance from the populace? If the optimum use of a personal life is for the greater good of others, and if maximizing life for achievements that extend beyond yourself is to influence and elevate others, then who holds the best standard? Who are the contestants in our search for qualified leadership, who are worthy of our reverence and imitation? Is it Washington, Lincoln, Churchill or Mandela? Is it George Washington Carver, Rosa Parks, Martin Luther King Jr.? Is it a scientist such as Sir Isaac Newton? Or an artist of the caliber of Rembrandt? Or is it perhaps a famous religious leader such as Pope John Paul II, Gandhi or the Dalai Lama?

Who is ultimately worthy of your full allegiance?

For me, I keep coming back to the perfect man Jesus, God's incarnate Son, who though he was tempted in all things as we are, was without sin.[1] I know of no one else in world history who has accomplished more from his life than Jesus of Nazareth. I know of no one more revered or pure, who demonstrated more integrity. For me, his life represents the best model for living an honorable and accomplished life.

And when I consider the life of Jesus, looking for the one

pivotal event that set the course of his life, showing both his inner strength and outward resolve in the face of unparalleled challenges, I think of his trial of temptation in the wilderness.

> Jesus, full of the Holy Spirit, returned from the Jordan and was led by the Spirit in the desert, where for forty days he was tempted by the devil. He ate nothing during those days, and at the end of them he was hungry.
>
> The devil said to him, "If you are the Son of God, tell this stone to become bread."
>
> Jesus answered, "It is written: 'Man does not live on bread alone.'"
>
> The devil led him up to a high place and showed him in an instant all the kingdoms of the world. And he said to him, "I will give you all their authority and splendor, for it has been given to me, and I can give it to anyone I want to. So if you worship me, it will all be yours."
>
> Jesus answered, "It is written: 'Worship the Lord your God and serve him only.'"
>
> The devil led him to Jerusalem and had him stand on the highest point of the temple. "If you are the Son of God," he said, "throw yourself down from here. For it is written:
>
> "'He will command his angels concerning you
>   to guard you carefully;
> they will lift you up in their hands,
>   so that you will not strike your foot against a stone.'"
>
> Jesus answered, "It says: 'Do not put the Lord your God to the test.'"
>
> When the devil had finished all this tempting, he left him until an opportune time. (Luke 4:1-13)

Alfred Edersheim, in his classic work *The Life and Times of*

Jesus the Messiah, helps us understand that Jesus was the singular representative of God's moral perfection who proved his credibility to both represent the Father and proclaim his revelation by enduring successfully the most intense battle of temptation imaginable. If he really was the perfect moral person, who was also destined one day to rule a perfect form of government known as the kingdom of God, he must of necessity pass the litmus test of standing against the most alluring alternatives to his own assignment. He had to validate his authenticity and right to rule by resisting the most intense form of temptation with which a man can be assaulted. He must be perfect.

Edersheim states:

> It is quite true that long previous biblical teaching . . . must have pointed to temptation and victory as the condition of spiritual greatness. It could not have been otherwise in a world hostile to God, nor yet in man, whose conscious choice determines his position. No crown of victory without previous contest, and that proportionately to its brightness; no moral ideal without personal attainment and probation.[2]

He's right. That's it. For a man to be truly great he must prove he can muster all his physical, emotional and spiritual resources to ward off an assault against his convictions—an assault so compelling that a less disciplined person would be overwhelmed by the sheer persuasiveness of the attraction and succumb. The proven leader must overcome the trial that threatens to capsize him before he completes his noble voyage. Shortcuts to greatness are offered to all of us. We are regularly given promises of achieving our results by using cheaper and less expensive means. However, that is never true when quality and integrity are at stake.

Precious stones and gems are formed by the greatest pressures that earth can provide. Glass, however, is molded in a moment by human fabrication. But glass also fractures at the simplest jarring, whereas a diamond is strong enough to cut the glass human hands have made. And the earth's precious stones are unparalleled in their intrinsic beauty. Indeed, even their unique value is due to the fact that they are rarely available; few have withstood the pressures of earth, and fewer still have been found.

And so it is with nobility. It is formed by withstanding the weight of stressful pressures far greater than ourselves. No noble person is ever formed by a life of relative ease and pleasure. So it was in the life of Christ.

At this inaugural stage of his life mission (ministry) he is confronted by all the dark powers of the evil world—from Satan himself. And the outcome of this great stress is a person whose unique value is apparent to us all.

No Mere Mortal

If we could view Jesus as just a man for a second, I want you to see that there are two forces at work in his life. One is the power of God in the person of the Holy Spirit, which is at work in him. The other is the power of evil in the person of the devil, which is at work outside of him. These two persons, active in the life of every true Christian, are always at odds with each other, and for a very simple reason.

The Holy Spirit, simply put, is the living, invisible presence of God. God, we learn from Scripture, is pure, perfectly holy, omnipresent and unequivocally focused on good. God cannot deny his nature—that would be an impossible contradiction—so it follows that the Holy Spirit is always pushing us to be good and do good as well. If he is inside of us (and Scripture tells us that is, in fact, the case for every Christian),[3] then we have all the power we need to make decisions for moral good.

On the other hand, the devil, the moral antitheses to God, is immoral, impure and evil. Scripture teaches us that the devil (Greek *diabolos*, "slanderer," "accuser") is a created being with a distinct personality who chose to rebel against God's authority. He willfully chose to assail the purposes of God and, as a result, God banished him to an existence of his choosing—corrupt, devious, evil and expelled from the presence of God. The devil, Satan ("hater," "enemy," "adversary"), is now actively engaged in complete opposition to God. And he strategizes to seduce humankind to follow suit. If "God is love,"[4] then Satan is hate. If God is truth,[5] then Satan is a liar[6] and so forth.

So this diabolical fiend and friend of no one would naturally concentrate all the evil powers available to him in an attempt to destroy the redemptive plan of God before it even got started. If Satan could seduce and destroy Jesus, the Savior of humankind, then God's saving purposes would be defeated at the fountain-head, and all humankind would be lost. The devil would thereby be the victor.

So in this passage in Luke's Gospel, the devil is out to destroy Jesus. He wants to stop Jesus before Jesus gets started on his life mission. But he will try to trip up Jesus subtly. Satan will target Christ according to his needs, position and purpose—just as he does you and me.

All of this spiritual suspense brings us to our present study in the life of Jesus.

The account of Christ's struggle with the devil is critical for every believer. It shows both the credibility of God's kingdom representative as well as a method that we can employ for similar success against the temptation we face from the same adversary.

Notice first in the passage that the Holy Spirit led him into this time of temptation, and notice that it was in a desert after a forty-day interval of fasting. Jesus must have been weak and hungry and willing to do almost anything for a meal. Don't you think so? Fortunately, God's Spirit was with him as a fortifying companion.

From these verses you and I can quickly pick up some principles of truth for our own defense against the devil.

First, every Christian will encounter temptation—no matter how mature or long in the faith. If the devil tempted Jesus, then you can be sure that we are targets too. But every Christian will also have God's presence at each moment of temptation and God's power to see us through it successfully. God will allow each of us to be tempted,[7] but he also provides a way out so that we may be able to endure it. We only fall for the temptation, according to Scripture, when we desire the thing that Satan offers and pursue it in disregard for what is right. When we do this, we willfully reject God's escape, being overcome by the attraction of the bait and our desire for it.

Jesus' half-brother James reveals something of this desire when he writes, "When tempted, no one should say, 'God is tempting me.' For God cannot be tempted by evil, nor does he tempt anyone; but each one is tempted when, by his own evil desire, he is dragged away and enticed. Then, after desire has conceived, it gives birth to sin; and sin, when it is full-grown, gives birth to death" (James 1:13-15). Notice he says we are carried away and enticed by our own evil desire, our own desire to obtain, our lust. Lust is simply desire out of control. Because God created us, every desire we have has a satisfying limit that keeps us in the bounds that God intended for us. Anything else is an unhealthy desire, in other words, something other than what God intends for us.

One commentator on the Bible helps explain this issue by writing that

> when the Bible says "by his own desire," the word "desire" merely means anything which attracts you, anything for which you have an earnest desire. When you desire food, that's good; but if you permit that desire for food to cross the barrier of self-control, you sin with gluttony. Every single desire is God-given. . . . Each temptation always preys upon a God-given desire and seeks to push it into sin in one of two directions. First, by pushing the God-given desire to exceed its normal limits into excess. Second, by pushing the God-given desire to find fulfillment in "off-limits areas."[8]

Second, we see how temptation was heightened after a period of austerity. There is nothing quite like being without something, especially if it's a perceived need, to make us more susceptible to the offer to have it. Satan knows that, and therefore it is one of his more seductive ploys.

For example, I try not to shop when I am hungry because I tend to buy more food than I need. Why? Because my defense system is a little weaker when my hunger is higher. The same idea carries over to other temptations. If your financial situation is strained and you're hungrier than normal for some fresh cash flow, beware the deals you are offered or investments you consider; it's easier to make a mistake. The same holds true for relationships. If you are hungrier than normal for intimacy because something isn't quite right at home, then I caution you to beware the women in your office or in your business meetings on trips away from home. There is enough sin nature in all of us to produce desire for the wrong things, especially if we are in a time of spiritual drought. Therefore, we need to know ourselves, recognize our weaknesses, flee the enticement and not flirt with our own selfish appetites. Instead, we must be vigilant against the subtle seduction of our adversary, the devil, and apply the power of God to our situation in order to experience his deliverance. That's the only way to experience victory, and that is just what Jesus did.

Notice the areas he was tempted in as well as his method for gaining victory. They are completely applicable to us.

Preservation

All of us have an innate desire to make it in life, to survive. We are also consciously aware of the basic components of life. We all need food, water, air and affiliation or relationship. Jesus knew it and the devil knew it, and that is exactly where the test starts. The devil asks Jesus (tempts him) to use his divine power to re-create the stones surrounding him by turning them into bread in order to satisfy his hunger through self-determination.

This is a very subtle temptation. At first it seems reasonable enough—Christ is hungry, he has the power to change things, why not do it? But he had made a commitment that precluded self-sufficiency and independent decision-making. He was in partnership with God the Father. He had agreed to follow the Father's lead. He didn't have permission from the Father, plus the temptation was also a subtle insinuation that his Father wasn't taking good care of him and was AWOL on this particular assignment. Jesus would have none of it. He had agreed to come to earth to represent the Father's interests and be in complete submission to his authority, plan and timetable. Christ would be the redeemer of all humanity. Here he would validate his right to be creation's Lord and reigning King—but he would do it the Father's way[9] and only as the power of the Holy Spirit enabled him.

So the test was not about a mere meal but about who was in

control of his life. "What does the heavenly Father want for my life right now? Is he capable of providing sufficiently, particularly when things appear so bleak?" That's the test of preservation.

We will all face the same decision. It is normally not as dramatic, but the issue is the same. If you are a Christian, then you have a contract with God to follow his lead. He has promised to take care of you.[10] You and I are supposed to trust God to provide. After all, he made the promise; we didn't. We do this by pursuing his source of provision within the parameters he has set for our life. If you are employed as an accountant, then God will provide for you within your role as an accountant.

But the challenge comes when some unexpected event occurs that jeopardizes our welfare. It's tempting to panic and beg, borrow or steal to satisfy our need with hardly a thought to consider what God might have in store for us and how he might provide, guide and instruct. Actually, it is amazing how with a little prayer and patience we can learn God's way of escape without our creating another problem by pursuing the wrong solution—which the devil sent our way.

And where did I come up with this answer? The same place Jesus did—from the Word of God. Scripture is always the way we defeat the temptation of our adversary, the devil. Knowing where to go to get the answer is a function of personal study or counsel with a godly Christian. But the answer is always there. And remember, since God can't deny his own attributes, then he is bound by his own reputation to adhere to his own statements on how he will take care of us.

Possessions

The second temptation is both subtle and common. Jesus was next asked by the devil to worship him in the place of God. Of course, there is a tradeoff. The devil offered a substitute for the Father's plan for Jesus to inherit the kingdom. Instead of taking the avenue of a suffering redeemer, Satan offered Jesus a cheaper and more expedient alternative—to simply worship him in defiance of God. Jesus could have his kingdom without any of the hassle; he only had to deny his own identity and switch his allegiance from the Creator God to the created and corrupted devil. Our Lord saw through this one too. As quickly as the temptation was given, it was summarily rejected as Christ once again quoted from Scripture, providing both his answer as well as moral equilibrium for himself.

I can't help but be impressed. Here again I find so many of us susceptible to this form of temptation. Who among us has not done the wrong thing in order to gain some temporary advantage, worldly possession or position? For some it's stealing; for others it's lying. Some have overworked, ignoring wife and children, to earn that little extra in order to buy that (you fill in the blank). And on a very low level, that's a form of wrong worship.

How so, you ask? Well, if worship is attributing our highest admiration, respect and loyalty to a thing and subjugating all feeling, actions and thoughts to its perspective, then to deny that perspective is to redirect some degree of worship. So if God calls us to care for our families as a moral outcome of giving him our full allegiance (worship), then to deny our families in order to gain a new set of golf clubs—or whatever—is to worship the wrong thing. And guess who sent this amoral or immoral alternative? That's right; it's the devil. And without even realizing it, we just turned in his diabolical direction. It makes you kind of angry, doesn't it? Like you just got ripped off? Well, we have all done it.

The important thing is to recognize it and see how we can

prevent such stumbles by living according to the Word of God. Like Christ, we need to know God's Word and apply it consistently to our lives. Sometimes that means waiting on God to provide for us according to his timetable and patiently waiting until he does.

Presumption

The third and final temptation has to do with risk. The devil, after seeing Jesus overcome the temptations by relying on the Word of God, throws our Savior a curveball by using the Word of God to tempt him. The devil challenges Jesus to do a risky thing—jump off the temple in order to prove that God's Word works.[11]

Our Lord saw through the devil's misinterpretation of Scripture and quoted another Old Testament passage to correct his adversary. Jesus based his decision on the universal principle that the created are not to presumptuously test the Creator's loyalty.[12]

The devil had misapplied Scripture, but Jesus noticed the error. God does tell us that he will protect us,[13] but God doesn't say that he will limit the consequences of our actions when they are in violation of a revealed truth. In other words, we all know that the law of gravity reveals the truth that all objects fall to earth—so it would be presumptuous to take a verse that says God will protect us from time to time from inadvertent accidents and twist it to mean that he will enable us to fly after jumping from the top of a tall building.

Incredibly, we do just that at times. We jump off buildings—without parachutes—when we enter into financial commitments we can't really afford. Sometimes the risk is in the friendships we keep, believing that we can hang with the wrong people and go to the wrong places, and it won't ultimately affect us. Sometimes we take a risk on a business partner when we really haven't established that we share the same values. Sometimes we risk our kids by not paying attention to their friends, entertainment or Internet access until it is too late.

Our God wants to prevent us from making these and other mistakes. He has given us ample guidance and information in his Word, the Bible. Also, God will provide warnings by his Spirit[14] throughout the decision-making process, as well as a safety door of escape.[15] But he does not rescue us from foolish decisions or their consequences until we have learned our lesson well—to live by his Word alone.[16]

So Jesus passed every test and now his moral right to lead was validated and strengthened. But what about you and me? You know that each day we are assaulted with various temptations. Some days are worse than others, but every temptation we give in to weakens us a little more, while every temptation we overcome strengthens us. I appreciate what one author reminds us of as he remarks:

> Someday, in the years to come, you will be wrestling with the great temptation, or trembling under the great sorrow of your life. But the real struggle is here, now. . . . Now it is being decided whether, in the day of your supreme sorrow or temptation, you shall miserably fail or gloriously conquer. Character cannot be made except by a steady, long continued process.[17]

I suppose President Clinton's impeachment was the final act in a long drama of sexual self-indulgence. His caving in to the desire to appease his lust finally caught up to him. Though it didn't change his position professionally, I think it did historically. He will always be remembered for his personal, moral failures rather than his significant policy achievements.[18]

And the result is that, though most Americans would not

impeach him, few admire his character. Unfortunately, the legacy he leaves will be smudged by this stain of moral indiscretions.

I am sure you, like me, want to be remembered for overcoming temptation and living above the moral mediocrity of our generation. Since we do, we will have to be vigilant in order to overcome the seductions of our permissive world and the desires inherent in our sin natures. We certainly must learn to recognize the reality and strategies of the devil and to be careful of our appetites, particularly in a time of austerity. We especially need to be students of the Scripture so that we can both know and use God's truth to guide us through the wilderness of competing influences on our lives. Then and only then will God be the true source of our security as we struggle with the issues of preservation, possessions and presumption.

May you, in Christ, find the moral strength to stand firm.

3

MISSION

Proceeding with a Purpose

LUKE 4:14-30

*R*ecently I have been inspired by the life of Nelson Mandela. A few weeks ago I knew nearly nothing about him except that he won world acclaim as a leader in the antiapartheid movement. Now, after reading a short biography of his life, I am impressed with his overwhelming sense of purpose. Mandela was in prison for nearly thirty years for his role in resisting segregation and racism in South Africa. Yet Mandela, always a controversial figure, won the 1993 Nobel Peace Prize for his role in the establishment of inclusive democracy in his homeland. It was the capstone to the process to which he had dedicated himself for nearly four decades.

Though controversial, what inspires me is that his life exhibited tireless dedication to certain values he held as inviolable.

As a result, he organized all of his personal habits to ensure his progress toward his one overriding goal: democracy for all South Africans.

Nelson Mandela is known for his discipline, punctuality, emphasis on education, boundless energy and personal integrity. As one author comments:

> The years in jail reinforced habits that were already entrenched: the disciplined eating regimen of an athlete began in the 1940's, as did the early morning exercise. Still today, Nelson Mandela is up by 4:30 a.m. irrespective of how late he has worked the previous evening. By five he has begun his exercise routine that lasts at least an hour. Breakfast is by 6:30 when the day's newspapers are read and his work begins. With a standard working day of at least 12 hours time management is critical. Nelson Mandela is extremely impatient with unpunctuality regarding it as insulting those you are dealing with.[1]

This guy is one focused individual. That challenges me. But one characteristic about his leadership stands out above the rest. After years in prison, an environment that would sap the confidence of normal men, Mandela still had the inner resolve and confidence to pursue his dream of an integrated society and democratic government in South Africa. That sense of purpose expressed through his personal disciplines led to a strategy that ensured that democracy would prevail for black Africans in the white-ruled South African government. So in 1994, when he was inaugurated as the first democratically elected president of South Africa four short years after his release from prison, vindication for Mandela's sense of purposefulness was sealed.

These are the kinds of characteristics that inspire me. Purposeful people with tireless discipline are the kind of people I am motivated to follow. And that is the type of leadership I want to display as well, not because I want to grunt and groan like an overtaxed weightlifter through life, but because I do not want to be distracted from worthy goals and blocked by adversaries from achieving what's best for me and others. People who know where they are going in life and why inspire me. I am also determined to have a sense of direction in my own life; apparently others feel the same way.

Bill Walton, the former basketball great, spoke on the behalf of United States Democratic presidential candidate Bill Bradley at a Boston fundraiser in 1999 during Bradley's campaign. I was surprised at how admirably Walton spoke of his former opponent. He extolled Bradley's on-court leadership, his natural sense of how to win, his reliability and his perseverance. Bill Walton thought highly of Senator Bradley and was prepared to follow him. Therefore, he told his audience, he was privileged to give a glowing endorsement for the senator's bid to become the next president of the United States.

People follow those who have a sense of purpose, who demonstrate an innate directional focus that not only guides their way but also tests every option and opportunity that the leader encounters. As you watch a gifted leader, you will see that every decision is made by taking into account what value an option or opportunity would provide to the leader's overall purpose. If it's minimal compared to other options, it will be rejected just as surely as a contradictory option would. The definitive leader understands the costs and consequences of his decisions but accepts them as necessary payment for the privilege of pursuing a greater goal.

Today it's not easy to find a man of influence with the determination, self-discipline, vision and courage to seek his goals with single-mindedness. Rarer still is the man who has a solid biblical basis for his objectives and a sense of God's commissioning to his life's pursuits.

Fortunately, we still have the model of Jesus. I know of no more focused, principled, determined and self-sacrificing individual. It's no wonder that he still inspires followers so long after his death. His wisdom, compassion, integrity, commitment and accomplishments are unparalleled. He continues to inspire millions to pursue similar objectives. Some do so even at the cost of their lives.

When I consider the basic ingredients of being a follower of Christ, of being a Master's man, I realize that one of the most fundamental qualities is a sense of divine purpose. To follow Christ means similarly having a sense that God wants you to pursue a certain course of life. Jesus knew well his purpose. It was biblically inspired, and everything he said or did revolved around the faithful pursuit of that end. His purpose gave him a sense of direction, confidence, courage and satisfaction. Who could ask for more from a life? Who could want more from a model?

David Rockefeller once stated that "the number one function of a top executive is to establish the purpose of the organization."[2] Our Lord did exactly that, as Luke records in the fourth chapter of his Gospel.

> Jesus returned to Galilee in the power of the Spirit, and news about him spread through the whole countryside. He taught in their synagogues, and everyone praised him.
>
> He went to Nazareth, where he had been brought up, and on the Sabbath day he went into the synagogue, as was his custom. And he stood up to read. The scroll of the prophet Isaiah was handed to him. Unrolling it, he found the place where it is written:

"The Spirit of the Lord is on me,
   because he has anointed me
   to preach good news to the poor.
He has sent me to proclaim freedom for the prisoners
   and recovery of sight for the blind,
to release the oppressed,
   to proclaim the year of the Lord's favor."

Then he rolled up the scroll, gave it back to the attendant and sat down. The eyes of everyone in the synagogue were fastened on him, and he began by saying to them, "Today this scripture is fulfilled in your hearing."

All spoke well of him and were amazed at the gracious words that came from his lips. "Isn't this Joseph's son?" they asked.

Jesus said to them, "Surely you will quote this proverb to me: 'Physician heal yourself! Do here in your hometown what we have heard that you did in Capernaum.' "

"I tell you the truth," he continued, "no prophet is accepted in his hometown. I assure you that there were many widows in Israel in Elijah's time, when the sky was shut for three and a half years and there was a severe famine throughout the land. Yet Elijah was not sent to any of them, but to a widow in Zarephath in the region of Sidon. And there were many in Israel with leprosy in the time of Elisha the prophet, yet not one of them was cleansed—only Naaman the Syrian."

All the people in the synagogue were furious when they heard this. They got up, drove him out of the town, and took him to the brow of the hill on which the town was built, in order to throw him down the cliff. But he walked right through the crowd and went on his way. (Luke 4:14-40)

The organization Jesus founded was the church, that is, Christianity. Throughout his recorded life you see him execute a life mission targeted toward the establishment of a group of committed followers who would, in turn, perpetuate the same mission. And nowhere does he state his purpose more succinctly than in this passage of Scripture. As he does, he also shows us something of the response that similarly minded Christians can expect from the general public. Let's begin by looking at his first days in office, so to speak.

Positive Beginnings, Initial Success

Like many of us starting out on our career path, Jesus experiences a certain initial degree of success and affirmation. Think about your career path. Like most people, you probably have moved vocationally according to your gifts and the success the expression of those gifts has achieved. So it was with Jesus. Notice how nobly he began. He started his life's work filled with the presence and power of God.

By the way, today's Christian has the same presence of God to enable his or her life. God promises to reside in us too when we accept Christ as our Savior. And having accomplished that, God also empowers, teaches and leads us so that we too can achieve his highest ideals.[3]

Notice too that the man who pursues his profession as God directs and empowers him is a man who will gain the attention of others. So it was with Jesus. So it will be with you.

Our Lord's occupation was that of an itinerant teacher. His vocation was to preach. That's what he did. If he'd been an accountant, I'm sure he would have kept people's books accurately and executed the job with skill, integrity and proficiency. In fact, he performed his duties as a teacher so exceptionally that his professional accomplishments were advertised throughout the region by its citizens (Luke 4:14, 22). Most of us would love to have the same notoriety among our customers. We're gratified when people recognize our effort and pay tribute to our skills. And the fame can help us grow financially and professionally.

Typically, the career person who does well in his first position is quickly promoted. Perhaps his contract is renegotiated, and he's given an opportunity to transfer on to greater responsibilities on behalf of the company. And with the promotion come the trappings of success—a bigger office, his own secretary, greater flexibility over his schedule, a larger expense account, nice perks and more expectation to hang with other top dogs in order to rub shoulders with yet more potential clients who can help his company and himself move yet higher up the success ladder. And as he pushes through the barriers that prevent others from achievement, he must beware. There is a subtle temptation with career success.

From Christ's example I glean three dangers of deviation. The danger most common to initial career success is *to let the success go to your head* and begin to play to the applause instead of the original game. In this danger we suddenly forget our foremost mission. Blinded by the new attention and perhaps inflated with a new sense of confidence, we suddenly believe that the mission is to continue or to increase the applause. We begin to focus more on making our audience happy and less on fulfilling our original assignment. Slowly, subtly at first, but significantly we target pleasing others as the definition of success and deviate from our initial goal.

How often we have seen that tragedy occur in the life of a young athlete, movie star or business person who after a year or so in the spotlight finds himself or herself so busy signing autographs, fulfilling speaking engagements, endorsing products or accepting plaques and tributes that soon he or she is embarrassed by poor performance, brought on by these self-indulgent distractions. Don't let that happen to you. Enjoy your success, but always weigh the acclaim and referrals against your original commitment, and don't waver. Remember that life is a marathon and not a dash. Don't sprint off chasing some carrot until you assess how it relates to the fulfillment of your original purpose, how it affects your long-range plan.

Proclaiming the Gospel, Inviting Participation

Next we see Jesus return home as Luke moves our attention into the heart of this passage. After the initial success of his ministry following his baptism, wilderness temptation and preliminary teaching effort, Jesus returns to declare his life's work to his old neighborhood. In verse 16 Luke names Jesus' hometown and a clue is provided as to why this man had such a good sense of balance. His equilibrium was based on his personal habits and discipline, called "custom" in this passage.

And what was his custom? Apparently, as I read verses 17-20, it had several elements: (1) familiarity with Scripture, (2) regular attendance with other devout believers and (3) familiarity with God, who guides each life. Let me see if I can back that up.

Notice that he went, as was his practice, to the synagogue to worship. Notice that when he was handed the scroll, the long object of rolled paper on which was written the verses of the Old Testament Scripture, he was able to find a specific passage from which to read. Furthermore, after he quoted the verses, he announced confidently that this applied to him. That's amazing. I'm impressed. So was the crowd. But why? Because rare indeed is the man who can stand up in front of his peers and those who know him best and announce in unequivocal terms the conviction of what his life is all about. Rarer still is the man who can announce the basis of his life from a specific text of Scripture.

A clear, confident sense of direction, a bold sense of purpose inspires me. Doesn't it inspire you? I want to know where that kind of person is going and why. I find I am motivated to follow a person's agenda if it is loftier and more significant than mine.

When we examine the quotation Jesus used, we are given a clue to the identification of his life's mission. Where was he going? His target was to go out into the community to meet the needs of broken people and to proclaim the fact that God's deliverance was provided for their benefit. Why? Because God's Spirit had moved with such force in his heart that he couldn't do anything else and feel the same satisfaction and sense of accomplishment. Christ came to tell people the good news of God's love for them and his personal provision to pay the penalty of their sins. He proclaimed an unequaled message that God was providing the opportunity for people to have a renewed, intimate relationship with himself.

Christ came to provide practical help to the hurting by healing the sick, restoring sight to the blind and giving mobility to the paralyzed, purity to the immoral and emancipation to all those afflicted by bondage to sin.

Christ came to declare to us inmates that the cells have been opened, the bars removed and the guards eliminated. We are now, by Christ's coming, liberated from our slavery to sin and free to enjoy a relationship with God through him. Isn't that the greatest news you've ever heard? Don't you think the afflicted and tormented souls of this world must jump for joy at hearing the prospect of such a change of status?

No wonder he was passionate and focused. You would think that everyone would applaud and follow, but you'd be wrong. After their initial burst of enthusiasm, the people began to question his credentials. They had seen him grow up. They knew his family. They were familiar with his mother's questionable pregnancy, his father's modest employment and Jesus' lack of a formal education. What credentials are these? Who is he to preach to us? Who is he to lead? So they questioned his authority out loud.

This brings us to the second danger of deviation, which is *to forgo your sense of mission because of intimidation*. Most of us have experienced rejection. Most of us have been embarrassed at some point in our life. Do you remember raising your hand in class and enthusiastically giving a wrong answer? And do you remember the horror when your mistake was immediately pointed out by the hilarious laughter of your fellow students? You could just die, right? Or have you been caught singing in your car and stopped because of the glare of a neighboring motorist? We really care a lot about how people view us, don't we? The cosmetics industry proves that. We especially guard what we believe until we know we're in friendly company and won't be ridiculed or rejected for what we say or how we feel.

I think Jesus knew his neighbors. He was familiar with their mores, expectations, prejudices and sympathies. What Unionist in his right mind, for example, would try to repudiate the travesty of slavery to a group of Confederate sympathizers during the height of the Civil War? Well, that's essentially what Jesus did here. He said things that would shake up the status quo. Israel wanted deliverance from Rome, and military might, they believed, was the answer. They weren't interested in some spiritual dream announced by an uneducated carpenter. "Well, the audacity of that man." But Jesus said it anyway. He said it because it was right. He meant it because it was true. And he knew from Jewish history that his nation had a tendency to miss God's supernatural provisions during difficult times; so he confidently let his passionate message fly. He didn't care that some bystander might disapprove of his preaching.

How about you? Do you have the confidence to be passionate about your cause for Christ? Accountants can be passionate about Jesus and God's emancipating grace for sinners. So can engineers and school teachers and truck drivers and doctors and any other kinds of people you can name. Unfortunately, the bigoted want to maintain their position and the status quo. If they can't back you down through derision, they'll do it through intimidation—or, worse, by force.

Proving the Point, Identifying the Problem

Notice that after Jesus reminded them of their tendency to dismiss God's prophets, the crowd grew hostile. People don't like to be proved wrong when getting right means they have to deal with themselves.

Have you noticed that people prefer to mask their wrongdoing by hanging with wrongdoers of the same nature? I suppose that as "birds of a feather flock together," hard hearts do too. I sympathize with them. Frankly, it breaks my heart to see people so ignorantly reject the only thing that can help them. Misery likes company, I suppose, and collectively they give each other strength and motivation to mess up one more day. But get them alone and allow them to tell their story and soon the ice will melt and their soft core will show, and they'll tell you how miserable they've been and wonder if God really does care about them. After all, they have "been so bad for so long." Fortunately we can tell them yes. You may be a real screwup, but God still cares and loves and forgives and forgets. That's why he sent Jesus. He sent him just for them and us. He came to unlock the cell around their hard heart and to let them run free, right into the renewing arms of God. And with a message that incredible our Master wasn't about to be dissuaded by the uninformed.

You shouldn't either. Don't ever let your detractors hamper you. Remember their plight, what they seek to protect, and their fear of what they don't yet know. But also beware, because as a group they can back you up and make you shut up.

And that leads to our third danger of deviation: *to react to criticism and change your mission.* Don't do it. Don't be a lounge musician who changes his style of music to please the audience. Have the courage to do what you know is right. Have the courage to say what you know is true. And have the courage to continue. Jesus did. Notice the special stamina as well as the amazing deliverance God gave him when they tried to eliminate him by throwing him down a cliff. They wanted every vestige of what he represented out of their lives. And he gave them what they wanted by being true to his own sense of purpose. He left. However, note the wording of verse 30. Which way did he go? Was he persuaded to go their way? No, he went his way. Sadly for them, they lost their only true hope for a meaningful life. Happily for us, Jesus never deviated from pursuing the direction God entrusted to him until his mission was complete.

I know he calls his followers to do the same thing, but will we? Before we conclude this section, consider two reasons why this subject of having an overall purpose is important. Number one is *making decisions.* No matter what the issue is—marriage, children, career, geographic location, lifestyle, schools—if you align your decisions with your mission, they will aggregately and cumulatively lead you to your target. Number two is *making a difference.* If you invest your time, energy, talents and network toward your singular goal, then the experiences of your life will enable you to optimize your life achievements for a maximum impact according to your purpose.

And how do we know our purpose? Well, I suggest you try this process. You can roughly guess your purpose by looking at your life path and seeing where you have been a success, what you did that won you the respect and appreciation of others, and what it is that stirs your heart. That is, what are you passionate about? Now take that information and see if you can detect a pattern. If you can, you will probably have an immediate sense of confirmation. Then pray about it, asking God to confirm it in your heart and to seal the sense of purpose by providing you with peace internally. Now take the list of qualities, desires and accomplishments and write the first draft of a mission statement, trying especially to distill the information down to one overarching result that you seek to achieve in all that you do.[4]

Finally, you might ask a few close friends or family members if these qualities and the resulting statement seem to represent you accurately. If they agree, you should be assured by now of at least your general direction. If they add legitimate points, then integrate these into your self-analysis and restate your purpose accordingly.

This exercise might take several tries and probably won't be perfected for several years, but it will go a long way in helping you to identify what you are to do in life. Later God may provide a verse of Scripture that seems to sum up your passion. And armed with this kind of divine directional reinforcement, you will find a new confidence in pursuing your life goals.[5]

Now that we have a sense of where we are supposed to go, I think we stand a good chance of getting there. I can't think of a better way of knowing that I will end well than by beginning with that end in mind. How about you?

4

SOLITUDE

Necessary Times of Silence
LUKE 4:31-44

*D*o you remember your preschool naptime? I did not like slowing down as a kid, and I do not like slowing down now. However, what my mom knew then is a principle we need to learn today: no one can go full throttle indefinitely without burning out or, worse, crashing all together. Tim Hansel, in his book *When I Relax I Feel Guilty,* gives us this warning:

> Many of our sins are caused by hurry and thoughtlessness. No matter how good our purpose is, a driven man is still enslaved. He cannot act freely, thoughtfully, lovingly. . . . Quiet minds, which are established in stillness, refuse to be perplexed or intimidated. They are like a clock in a thunderstorm, which moves at its own pace.[1]

He's right. If a man isn't careful, the exhilaration of seeking to achieve will ultimately be eclipsed by the discouragement of lost motivation and direction. Dr. Richard A. Swenson, in his outstanding work on balance titled *Margins,* provides some further helpful reminders:

> Constant activity is a characteristic of our age. If we are not active, we feel slothful. If we are not productive, we feel guilty. . . . I am not saying that productivity is wrong. I am only saying it must not be idolized. . . . Work in our culture often dominates other areas of life. To be sure, work is very important. But other activities are more important.
>
> The people who work the hardest and rest the least naturally rise to the top, from where they drive the entire work system. They set the rules, which maximize productivity. Even love and relationship come far down the list. Little wonder rest cannot find a resting place. . . .
>
> When emotionally exhausted, the first thing I do is find quiet, solitude, and a chance to do nothing. I don't feel guilty, for the fallow times are just as important as productive times. I cycle quickly, and if depleted, my energy will return shortly. All I need is quiet and some time.[2]

Another group of doctors adds its support to the necessity of rest by commenting on burnout and the Type A personality:

> One of the most common definitions of burnout describes it as a loss of enthusiasm, energy, idealism, perspective, and purpose. It can be viewed as a state of mental, physical, and spiritual exhaustion brought on by continued stress.
>
> How much of a "Type A" personality are you?
>
> The medical profession defines a "Type A" personality as one who is time oriented and never seems to have enough time. He tends to be competitive and success-oriented, a workaholic, often doing two or more things at once.
>
> It is important for the Type A personality to slow down, relax,

and put priorities in proper order. Type A personalities tend to move, walk and eat rapidly. Since type A persons usually live life on a schedule—a tight schedule—they must rearrange that schedule to include time to relax, time with the Lord.[3]

I owe a lot to these men. Several years ago I found myself going full throttle with an overabundance of projects, all of which I loved. Besides my normally full schedule of ministry, I oversaw the designing and building of our dream home. I was also engaged in starting a citywide outreach ministry and writing another book. Without realizing it, I was headed for trouble fast. I was feeling dizzy a lot. My head pounded all the time. Tylenol, Rolaids and coffee kept me going. Sleep was at a minimum, and the stress from things going wrong enabled me to choose to keep myself in a constant state of smoldering anger. After I nearly fainted a couple of times and discovered a numbness in my left arm, I finally went to a doctor who is a friend and fellow church member.

Dr. Jones (honestly that is his name) told me that I was a candidate for either a heart attack or more likely a stroke. He chewed me out pretty good, told me to lose some weight and then gave me a prescription for some long overdue medicine— a week's vacation with my family. I am not kidding! I couldn't remember the last time we had a week off together—maybe seven years? This time of overextended work in my life was literally jeopardizing my life—me, an ardent athlete and outdoorsman who never got sick and got my thrills from hyperdrive achievement.

Thanks to my wife, my doctor and these fine authors I got the help I needed to realign my perspective with reality and restore some balance and ultimately some health in my life. I didn't think workaholism and the resulting poor health would ever happen to me. But the pursuit of some awesome ministry goals, the development of a new organization, the design and construction of our new home, and an addiction to the adrenaline rush of all of this effort brought me to the brink of disaster and taught me some important lessons. I have found that the downside of success is stress, a stress that creeps imperceptibly higher as we gradually increase our responsibility to keep up with the ever-increasing demands for our service.

Think about some accomplished professionals. They get our attention. On the one hand they inspire us to seek heights of personal achievement that we didn't dream possible. On the other hand we recognize their unique gifts and realize that we can't ever really copy them, so we applaud them and follow.

And it happens on every level and stratum in society. No matter where you are and who you are looking up to, there is always someone beneath you—younger, less experienced, less talented, looking up to you, appreciating you, following your example, and pressing you to stretch further. It is gratifying, but it is also tiring. And that is the subtle danger of success and accomplishment. You are never done. People always want more, and the better you do, the more you are asked to do.

And that is where we find ourselves in this passage with Jesus. Here we shall see Jesus successful, busy, interrupted, followed and put upon. His ministry success has earned him more demands for his service, and something has got to give—even for the Son of God.

> Then he went down to Capernaum, a town in Galilee, and on the Sabbath began to teach the people. They were amazed at his teaching, because his message had authority.
>
> In the synagogue there was a man possessed by a demon, an evil spirit. He cried out at the top of his voice, "Ha! What do you

want with us, Jesus of Nazareth? Have you come to destroy us? I know who you are—the Holy One of God!"

"Be quiet!" Jesus said sternly. "Come out of him!" Then the demon threw the man down before them all and came out without injuring him.

All the people were amazed and said to each other, "What is this teaching? With authority and power he gives orders to evil spirits and they come out!" And the news about him spread throughout the surrounding area.

Jesus left the synagogue and went to the home of Simon. Now Simon's mother-in-law was suffering from a high fever, and they asked Jesus to help her. So be bent over her and rebuked the fever, and it left her. She got up at once and began to wait on them.

When the sun was setting, the people brought to Jesus all who had various kinds of sickness, and laying his hands on each one, he healed them. Moreover, demons came out of many people, shouting, "You are the Son of God!" But he rebuked them and would not allow them to speak, because they knew he was the Christ.

At daybreak Jesus went out to a solitary place. The people were looking for him and when they came to where he was, they tried to keep him from leaving them. But he said, "I must preach the good news of the kingdom of God to the other towns also, because that is why I was sent." And he kept on preaching in the synagogues of Judea. (Luke 4:31-44)

It is the same for you. You can't turn the spigot off without hurting your clients and your reputation and vocational progress. But you need to anyway or you will eventually lose all of your momentum and be forced to sit it out due to burnout. So you need to slip silently away from the spigot for a brief period of rest. It is the cost of success. Recognize it and resign yourself to it. You are not going to slow down later, so you must rest when you can.

How can we maintain our equilibrium in the busying pace of success? First, by maintaining our focus on our mission. But something more is needed. We need to get closer to the center of our life.

When I was seven or eight, we lived next to an abandoned elementary school. It was a great place to play. The schoolrooms were locked and boarded up—good, who needs 'em? But the playground equipment was fully intact. That was a pleasant present to us neighborhood kids. The best piece of equipment in the yard was the merry-go-round. It was a crude contraption of welded metal, a floor, rails to hang onto and a center pole around which it revolved. It was totally kid powered. We all took turns rotating the thing for our friends. They would climb on board and grab the rails, and we would run along the side pushing as hard as we could. The hoped-for climax was to get the thing spinning so fast that a kid or two would slip off, being spun into the schoolyard, or maybe someone would get sick and throw up. The bigger kids relished the thrill and challenge of hanging onto the rails and hanging out beyond the platform in order to experience maximum Gs. The smaller ones were taught to quit crying by slowly moving to the center of the merry-go-round. We found that the closer to the center you got, the more stability you enjoyed no matter how fast the thing was going.

That is still an important principle for a Master's man. Gentlemen, the faster your life goes, the more focused you must also be on your center if you are to survive—not to mention thrive. And what or who is the center of your life? It's not your favorite football team or even your family. It certainly isn't your career and shouldn't be your golf game. It's God. He created you. He provides life and health and happiness to you. He guides and provides, protects and corrects. He is the center of your life.

Everything revolves around him just as the planets do the sun.

But we often forget, or at least neglect, that fact. And due to the exhilaration of our ride or sheer panic from its velocity, we hang on for dear life but never slow down enough to stabilize. We need to rest and catch our breath by drawing closer to the center, to God. It's time we use physics to our advantage. It's time we use common sense. It's time we realign our activities around the security of that perfect center. If you're not convinced that we should, a brief section of Scripture shows how important this issue was to our Lord.

Even the Perfect Man, Jesus, saw the need for renewing his relationship with the Father in order to succeed in his earthly responsibilities. If Christ needed the recalibration, rest and renewal that come from solitude, I believe we need them more.

Let me use that word *solitude* to encompass the concept of realignment with God. God doesn't often shout to get our attention. More often than not he whispers.[4] And by design his whispering necessitates times of quiet if we're to hear his voice. The noisier, crazier and faster your life is, the less chance you have of hearing him. The only recourse you have is to draw away from the activities to a quieter place of solitude. There you can offer your concerns to him in prayer and become receptive to hearing his direction to you through his Word. Our Lord was a master at this discipline. Let's notice how he operates. Let me introduce you to the busiest recorded day in the life of our Savior.

Luke 4:31-44 is a relatively short section of Scripture, but it is very busy. In fourteen short verses we catch about twenty hours of a day in the life of Jesus. Look at the details with me.

First of all, we see him at the synagogue worshiping. It's the sabbath, a holy day of rest as prescribed by God and published by Moses in the Ten Commandments. If you're like me, that represents the one day I don't want any outside interference.

No intrusions from work interrupting my rest, repose and football, please. But Christ wasn't afforded that luxury. In the midst of the sermon a crazy man stood up and caused a scene. Actually, he was demon-possessed and presented a formidable challenge to the believing community. The man spouted off something to Jesus that seemed to malign his intent in ministry, but our Lord, with all the authority of the Godhead, simply cast the obnoxious intruder out of the person and sent the demon packing while sending shock waves of amazement through the audience. Here our Lord as Messiah and Savior demonstrates the authority and power that was inherently his as God. It was an impressive display of God's pity on beleaguered humanity while repulsing the assault of an emissary of our adversary the devil.

Let's digress a moment to underscore an important principle. All of you men are men of influence to one degree or another. You certainly are teachers in your home, and many of you are leaders in business, politics, ministry and other affairs. And, like Christ, you will have challenges to your authority from others. I appreciate the man who can extend mercy to those beneath him though they tire him with their assaults. But at some point we must exercise our authority through appropriate discipline or else order breaks down. And, like Christ, it must be done with power. We need to discipline (without severity) our children, reprimand errant employees and stand strongly against those who promote evil in our society. It isn't fun. It may be difficult, but at some point it's necessary or we have no authority at all. We'll find ourselves rulers of nothing.

Now back to the text. Synagogue worship is over, and it's off to lunch at Simon's house. But as the distinguished guest arrives, he finds another matter that needs his attention before he can eat. Simon's mother-in-law is sick, and Jesus is asked to attend to her. So Jesus spontaneously treats her, and her healing is so complete that she is able to resume her duties as hostess, and the mealtime goes forward.

However, now a crowd begins to gather at the door requesting yet more time and attention from Jesus. Luke records that this third request for our Lord's professional services lasted well into the night. How do we know that? Because of two things. One, because this was the Jewish sabbath. The people were forbidden by Jewish religious law from traveling long distances. The Jews reckoned time differently than the Romans, whose time we've adopted. Instead of a new day beginning just after midnight, the Jewish day ran from 6 p.m. to 5:59 p.m., or about sundown to sundown. Second, since the healing service didn't begin until sometime after sundown, and noting the volume of people as well as the fact that Christ "was laying his hands on each one," we can imagine it was quite late before he turned in.

Ever have a day like that? It begins normal enough, but every expectation for normalcy is dashed as one crisis after another pops up, and you are the only one who can handle it. And before you know it, it is well into the evening before you can call it a day. Yes, I know some of you, due to your responsibilities, live like this day after day. That's the way it goes for the successful. The more you do, the more you're requested to do. And soon fatigue, frustration and perhaps even failure creep in.

Jesus knew how to prevent this downward spiral. He crawled closer to the center of his merry-go-round. He drew nearer to God by getting alone with him. For Jesus it was early in the morning,[5] and notice that it didn't last long. What about us? If we're busy, do we even see the need for such a time of spiritual reflection with our Savior as the Master saw the need to spend time with the Father? And if we do see the need, are we taking the time? Even if it's just a little?

Also, I notice that our Lord took what time he had and let it go at that. It wasn't, this day, a four-hour prayer time, but he at least took some time. I want you to be encouraged by this. I believe this passage acknowledges that it is unrealistic to think that we men are always going to be able to spend lots of uninterrupted time sitting quietly before the Lord, pondering the meaning of life. Some days you may be able to, but most days you won't. The passage's point, I believe, is to take time with the Lord, and the only way to do that is to make time for the Lord, however brief that may need to be due to inevitable interruptions. Busyness is no excuse for not having a relationship with God. We still must maintain him as our primary source of energy and focus for life. To do that we need to take time with him whenever we can, whether it's in the car as we're on the way to work or to appointments, before others in the home get up, or at night when they've gone to bed.

I see in this passage the same kind of flexibility and determination modeled by the Master. He took a brief devotional break, before his schedule took over his day, with his Father. Afterward he continued his professional responsibilities according to his mission. That motivates me. I know my life gets out of control, and now I know how to get back in control. I need some time with God, some time in prayer, some time in Scripture, some time when I won't be distracted or interrupted. I need some solitude, even if it's brief. And it is nice to know that it works.

I don't know about you, but for me the morning is best. But whether I am at home, in the car, on the way to work or in the house when the family has gone to bed, I make sure I catch a little time with God and restore balance by moving toward the center. Also, I learned years ago that the beckoning of my sports and business page were louder than my Bible, so I canceled the morning paper, knowing that I had a strong competitor for the precious spiritual time I needed first thing in the morning. I'm able to catch up with sports and business at lunch.

This plan may not work for you, but I know it's best if you have some sort of time with your Savior during the day. There are lots of helpful tools available for a daily devotion that can provide a little helpful structure to get you on the way. I suggest you look into something short, practical and relevant that has a verse of Scripture and maybe a comment related to the text and a short prayer as a minimum.

As we wind down our study in this chapter, consider with me these reminders concerning the significance of solitude. First, it's necessitated by success. Second, Satan will challenge it. So third, it must be purposely sought. As a result, you'll find solitude an antidote for stress.

And finally, this note. In these last three studies we've noticed three specific strategies that Satan uses to derail us from being men of God. The first is trial and temptation (chapter two), as we noticed in our Lord's wilderness temptations. The second is the problem of critics and cynics (chapter three), which we saw in the Master's efforts to express his mission to the people of his hometown. And in this chapter we saw the third strategy that Satan uses to derail us from being men of God: success and the demands that come from it.

Success is pretty heady stuff, but the only way we can keep our feet on the ground is to steady ourselves from its volume and velocity. We can do that by keeping our eyes focused on the real head of our life: the center of our universe, the Lord Jesus Christ.

5

TEAM

Recruiting for Fit

LUKE 5:1-11

I wasn't always a Dallas Cowboys fan. I grew up in Los Angeles, so the Rams were my team. At first they dominated the Cowboys, but it wasn't long until they began to lose consistently to Dallas—especially in big games. Roger Staubach & Co. ran over Roman Gabriel & Co. regularly. Then I moved to Dallas in the early eighties. Living in the enemy's hometown wasn't easy, but slowly I was converted. Why? It wasn't because the Dallas Cowboys kept winning. In fact, in Troy Aikman's first year they were 1 and 15. The reason I changed loyalties was because of the solidarity and integrity of the franchise. By solidarity I mean that the men who ran the organization had their act together. And by integrity I mean that the lead man, the out-front person, the coach, was a man of uncompromised values. Owner Clint Murchison, general manager Tex Schramm and head coach Tom Landry were a well-oiled team, and their united skillfulness permeated the entire

staff, front office, coaches and players. As a result of their una-
nimity and single-minded purpose, the Cowboys were consis-
tent frontrunners. And so they won my respect and admiration.
Years later I had the privilege of serving on the Dallas board of
the Fellowship of Christian Athletes with then-board chairman
Coach Landry. His coaching excellence and skill were evident
then as well. We too were a united, focused, single-minded
team.

What kind of guy is Jesus looking for to follow him? I think
he's looking for the same thing: men who are willing to submit
to his leadership, share his vision, catch his passion and integrate their skills into the whole toward the accomplishment of a
single, significant goal—the spiritual renewal of the world.

What characteristics did Jesus look for? What were his methods for recruiting? I believe the next section of Scripture gives
us at least part of the answer. Luke 5:1-11 reveals the invitation
he gave to Peter, James and John to become his followers. Later
there would be nine more through whom he would begin to
change the world.

One day as Jesus was standing by the Lake of Gennesaret, with
the people crowding around him and listening to the word of
God, he saw at the water's edge two boats, left there by the fishermen, who were washing their nets. He got into one of the boats,
the one belonging to Simon, and asked him to put out a little
from shore. Then he sat down and taught the people from the
boat.

When he had finished speaking, he said to Simon, "Put out
into deep water, and let down the nets for a catch."

Simon answered, "Master, we've worked hard all night and
haven't caught anything. But because you say so, I will let down
the nets."

When they had done so, they caught such a large number of

fish that their nets began to break. So they signaled their part-
ners in the other boat to come and help them, and they came
and filled both boats so full that they began to sink.

When Simon Peter saw this, he fell at Jesus' knees and said,
"Go away from me, Lord; I am a sinful man!" For he and all his
companions were astonished at the catch of fish they had taken,
and so were James and John, the sons of Zebedee, Simon's part-
ners.

Then Jesus said to Simon, "Don't be afraid; from now on you
will catch men." So they pulled their boats up on shore, left
everything and followed him. (Luke 5:1-11)

Robert Coleman, in his classic work *The Master Plan of Evangelism,* gives us an important insight into Christ's methods in
recruiting and developing into leaders the men he called. Coleman's words are worth repeating here.

What is more revealing about these men is that at first they do
not impress us as being key men . . . by any standard of sophisticated culture then and now they would surely be considered as a
rather ragged aggregation of souls. One might wonder how
Jesus could ever use them. They were impulsive, temperamental,
easily offended and had all the prejudices of their environment.
In short, these men selected by the Lord to be His assistants represented an average cross section of the lot of society in their
day. . . . Yet Jesus saw in these simple men the potential of leadership for the kingdom. They were indeed "unlearned and ignorant" according to the world's standard (Acts 4:13) but they were
teachable. . . . What perhaps is most significant about them was
their sincere yearning for God and the realities of His life . . .
these men were looking for someone to lead them in the way of
salvation. Such men, pliable in the hands of the Master, could be
molded into a new image—Jesus can use anyone who wants to
be used. . . . Jesus devoted most of His remaining life on earth to
these few disciples. He literally staked His whole ministry upon

them. The world could be indifferent toward him and still not defeat His strategy.[1]

So how was Christ to call them out? He used a very simple process. He personally selected them from the multitudes as he detected the qualities he could nurture to maturity. He perceived in these men the qualities requisite for representing him. Let's discover those qualities together as we pull the relevant details from this text.

Our account opens at a lake called Gennesaret, located in far north Palestine in the region where Jesus grew up. His base of operations was a city called Capernaum, which was on the lake, so he was probably not far from there as our passage begins.

Christ is teaching as a crowd of curious listeners begins to form. The time is approximately midmorning, since the text reveals that the fishermen are just in from their all-night fishing excursion. The timing is implied by the fact that the men are washing their nets before storing them in preparation for the next evening's work.

Anyone who's been on a lake knows how water amplifies sound. Many a time while bass fishing I could clearly hear entire conversations by people on the bank several hundred yards away. Since the crowd is gradually increasing in numbers and Christ intends for all to hear him clearly, he decides to use the natural amplification of the lake by preaching from a boat. Fortunately for him, he notices a fisherman nearby and requests his assistance by asking to borrow his rig. Our Master decides to use the boat as an aquatic preaching platform. The fisherman agrees, though he is busy and no doubt tired. Why? Has Jesus said something to pique his interest? Was the manner of Jesus so compelling that no one could refuse his sincere request? Who knows? But one fact is certain:

this was not the first time these two had met.

John's Gospel informs us that Simon,[2] the fisherman of our story, had previously spent the day with Jesus.[3] It seems Simon's brother was a follower of John the Baptist, and together they were looking for the Messiah of God. The prophet John was told he would recognize the Messiah by the appearance of a dove alighting on the person who came to be baptized. Recall that we reviewed this scene in chapter one. When the day came for Christ to inaugurate his ministry by undergoing the ritual of baptism, John saw the dove alight on Jesus. He knew, therefore, that Jesus was the Messiah and informed his disciple Andrew that "the Lamb of God, who takes away the sins of the world" (John 1:29) had arrived. John pointed him out to Andrew and another disciple who was standing nearby. These disciples were then introduced to Jesus, and they spent a day with him. The next day Andrew took his brother Simon to meet Jesus, and they spent another day together as well. It was during this visit that Simon was renamed Peter by Jesus. Apparently Simon Peter went back to his job as a fisherman, for the next time we see these men together is at the lake after the imprisonment of John the Baptist by Herod.[4] This is just before John the Baptist was beheaded.

Jesus, having recently migrated to the Sea of Galilee from the Jordan River, runs into Andrew and Peter, James and John, and invites them to follow him. Christ mentions at this time that he intends to modify their professional pursuits. They can keep fishing, but Christ wants it to be for people not fish. However, it seems the relationship is not solidified because we see Simon, James and John back at work at the lake (Luke 5:10). Here we pick up the story of their third meeting.

So again I ask, why did Jesus ask Peter, and why did Peter comply? I believe that for the first time Jesus was giving the fisherman an opportunity to assist in the work of the ministry and to do it in such a way that he could succeed. Jesus asked him to assist in a manner to which Peter could relate. Peter was familiar with the equipment, was in a position to loan it and saw the practical necessity of the request. Christ simply asked to use Peter's boat with the sturdy fisherman at the oars.

This, I believe, is our first clue to the kind of man Jesus was looking for to follow him. This introductory phase entails a feeling-out period, where a man can get to know Jesus without any risk to his current lifestyle just in case Jesus doesn't pan out. This phase includes some time together and, no doubt, information sharing. Certainly Peter was scrutinizing Jesus' words as he preached, and I believe Jesus was testing Peter to see if he would give him help in accordance with his current state of skill and resources. In other words, was the man available? Would he invest anything in developing the relationship? Would he hang out long enough to see what Christ is all about?

With that test completed, Christ applied a second test. He asked Peter to exercise faith. Peter was asked to risk failure and humiliation by trusting Christ to do the impossible—even the ridiculous. Jesus asked Peter to go back out onto the lake and fish again.

We need to understand what was at stake here. This seasoned fishing veteran, Peter, who made his living by knowing fish and optimal fishing conditions, was being asked by a religious teacher, a nonfisherman, to fish at the worst possible time of the day. Fishermen netted fish on the Sea of Galilee (that is, Gennesaret) at night when the air was cooler and the fish would rise to the surface to feed on baitfish. No one fished at midday, in the heat of the day, when the fish dove deep into cooler water. If they couldn't catch fish at night, in the most advantageous part of the day, what chance did they have now? Also, I am sure that Peter was tired from having been up all night. And perhaps of more concern was the fact that all of his neighbors and colleagues were standing on the beach watching this foolish effort.

But Peter did an amazing thing; he tried it. He complied with Jesus' request, although with some hesitation. Against his better judgment he rowed out into the middle of the lake and let down the nets. Of course, he didn't do it before first informing our Lord how unreasonable it was. But he did it nonetheless. And here lies the second characteristic our Master is looking for in men: Are we willing to trust him? Are we willing to risk ourselves by trying things his way?

Most of us struggle to trust Christ. First we have to get over the intellectual hurdle that he is really God. Then we have to get over the ego hurdle that we need his forgiveness by grace and can't earn it by effort. Then we have to get over the pragmatic hurdle of taking care of ourselves. After all, we're educated, experienced and have a track record that supports the concept that we know best how to run our lives.

At a shop for building Nascar Winston Cup racecars, I led a Bible study. The facility was located just north of Charlotte, North Carolina, at the offices of Dale Earnhardt, Inc. Until his recent death, Dale owned the #1, #8 and #15 Winston Cup cars as well as the #3 Busch Grand National car. It was a thrill being there because the men who worked there were seasoned professionals. Most of them were without any religious or academic pretenses. They only cared about what worked, and then once they found out what works, they immediately tried to figure out how they could make it better.

I'll never forget a study when I asked the question "Who takes care of you?" Without blinking one of the guys said, "I do. If I don't, nobody will." All the guys nodded in affirmation.

What followed was a spirited discussion of the fact that God takes care of you, and if he didn't, we'd evaporate in uncontrollable and insurmountable catastrophes. He controls the earth's climate, the air I breathe, the beat of my heart and, through his sovereignty, my job. Also, through his generosity and the facilitation of my employer, he provides my income, and so forth.[5] Sure we have the responsibility of instrumentality. That is, God uses our diligence, faithfulness and effort, but still, without him, we couldn't do a thing.[6]

Theologically his care and control are absolutely true, but practically we often think it's our education, skill, experience and effort that secure our welfare. As a result, it's really hard to trust God in the day-to-day practical matters, especially when you sense he's asking you to do something outside of your normal way of operation. But try we must, because that means we're trusting him, and trust (that is, faith) is the only way to succeed in the Christian life. It takes faith to be saved,[7] and it takes faith to succeed in pleasing God.[8] So faith is a crucial ingredient for a man who would follow Jesus.

But what does this faith look like? It looks like managing your money biblically and not by today's credit standards.[9] It means loving your wife and living with her in an understanding way instead of criticizing, demeaning and ignoring her.[10] It means raising your children biblically[11] and paying attention to their unique personhood[12] instead of raising them the way you were raised. It means being honest in business when cheating seems to work better and enable you to reach your goals faster. Faith means being willing to take the heat and bear the effort to do all the above right while waiting on the results because you believe what God said is true and that ultimately his way pays. Trust means knowing that he will come through even though you can't see how right now.

That's the kind of man Christ is looking for to follow him: a man who recognizes that Christ is the supreme authority, that the Master has all the power to accomplish what he purposes to do. So when he asks you to do something, he knows what he's about and you need to obey. Faith acknowledges that Jesus has the means to accomplish those results, and he's looking to you to provide the method. The Master wants you to be the man who rows the boat from which he creates the miracle in your life.

And what does such difficult faith net you? If the folks on the banks of the Sea of Galilee were laughing at Peter initially, they weren't ultimately. The text tells us that his ridiculous faith landed him such an abundance of good results that he had to call in reinforcements to haul up this great load of fish.

This leads us to the third quality for a follower of Christ, which is reverence. The word means respect, being able to appreciate the superiority of someone much greater than yourself. Luke writes that Peter, on seeing Christ do the impossible, the incredible, was struck by his unworthiness to be in the presence of One so powerful. Peter spontaneously confessed his unworthy nature and knelt before Jesus in worship.

I think faith and reverence go hand in hand. It's hard to trust someone you don't respect. Conversely, if you respect him, you'll trust him because you know (believe) he won't let you down.

How are you doing on this? Do you believe that Jesus is God? If so, then are you willing to trust him? Will you do what he says?

Probably the easiest way to test yourself on this point is to put into practice the things you already know that he wants you to do. If you don't know much about him, just read the New Testament and begin to apply it to your life. I guarantee you that he will treat you just like Peter. He will take your normal existence and make it incredible. The worst day fishing or working or living with Jesus beats the best day without him. He has the power to transform your life. He can do the incredible. He can take a normal vocation and make it spectacularly useful for his divine purposes just as he did Peter's that day.

By the way, I appreciate Christ's response to reverence. Notice his words in verse 10: "Don't be afraid." Christ didn't refuse Peter's reverence (worship), nor did he proclaim it inappropriate. No, he accepted it because he deserved it. And he deserves it from us too. But he isn't going to beat us up for our humanity. Christ is nothing if not a realist. He knows we blow it. He realizes we're imperfect; that's why he came to save us. But equally exciting is the fact that he accepts us just as we are. He isn't trying to intimidate us with his power. He isn't into rejection manipulation. He is trying to inspire us with his magnificence in order to get us to trust him. He wants to elevate the effectiveness of joy in our lives by working through us to do incredible things.

I know a man in Dallas who was born into a dysfunctional, alcoholic home in Galveston, Texas, who would tell you today, more than twenty-five years after Christ delivered him from all that, that he is amazed of what Christ is doing through him financially, professionally, philanthropically and relationally. Norm Miller has told me repeatedly how blessed—though unworthy—he is and what a thrill it has been and is to trust Christ. Norm's life is supercharged by God on behalf of Christ. And Christ wants us all to similarly experience his spiritual abundance.[13]

All of this leads us to the fourth and final characteristic of followers of Christ. They are dedicated. Jesus told the men that they would be going from catching fish, which soon died, to catching men alive (which is the literal translation of the Greek phrase used in Luke's text). How about that? Christ wants to take your very human existence and turn it into an eternally oriented one. In other words, whatever it is you do vocationally, socially, recreationally, etc., Christ wants to elevate its purpose in order to extend your influence eternally.

You may have a secular job, but Christ intends to use it for eternal effect. The Master wants men who, in the exercise of their profession, take note at how they can use it to influence people heavenward. We are to work and live and play in such a way as to influence others to take notice of our Savior so that they will gravitate toward him. Christ wants men and women to live, not die.

Every activity of life has a short life span, but if these activities are pursued in a way that the higher purpose of our Master is revealed, that something of his love and truth are expressed, then we find our old dead way of living (like those fish that men catch) will be transformed toward a way that brings life.

Only God can take a fisherman and make him a world changer as he did Peter. Much of the New Testament is written either about or by Peter, who became a great leader of the early church, and all because he reluctantly but willingly trusted Christ to do the impossible.

Don't let your current circumstances, past mistakes or future fears dissuade you from trusting Christ. It doesn't take much faith to see great results—just enough faith to try, to let down your nets for a catch. And the singular characteristic that will see you through a lifetime of trial, test and triumph is dedication. Christ is looking for men who will accept his invitation, lay aside old habits and follow him unswervingly.

The Master won't tell us where he's taking us, how we will get there or what will happen. He only asks us to follow. And the only word I know to use that encompasses the faith, commitment, courage and sacrifice to embark on such a journey, to become part of Jesus' team, is dedication.

Yes, I became a Cowboys fan after living in Dallas for a while. It wasn't because it was natural but because it was best. I was converted by the results. The Cowboys had a team that won more than they lost because they had leaders you could count on to perform. I'm a Christian now for the same reasons. Jesus Christ is a leader you can trust, and he is a Master you can't afford not to follow.

What do you think? Are you willing to consider being part of his team?

6

IMPACT

Ability Harnessed for Good
LUKE 5:12-26

*M*en of impact—such as Mark McGwire, Michael Jordan, Tiger Woods and Emmitt Smith—can take charge of the game single-handedly, dictate the outcome and ensure victory. Another name that comes to mind is Keith Phillips. Keith is not a sports hero, but I admire him all the same. His resolve has led to a game-turning effort sociologically and spiritually in America's inner cities. Keith, a UCLA graduate, has dedicated his life to serving the displaced minorities of America. Keith is founder and president of World Impact, a nationwide, interdenominational, Christian discipling and church-planting ministry dedicated to ministering God's love in the inner cities.

Keith began his work in 1965 in Los Angeles shortly before the Watts riots. His passion is to serve the impoverished, ethnically diverse communities in America that suffer from the worst of society's ills. Keith and his staff live in the heart of this economic wasteland known as America's inner cities. They work in an urban wilderness infested with drug addiction, prostitution, divorce, fatherless children, maternally run multigenerational families living on welfare or worse, and incomes produced by crime. These communities never make the ten most desirable places to live in America list, but they might make the worst ten.

World Impact staff live in the communities they serve, and as a result they often are robbed, harassed, ridiculed and threatened, but none of that matters to them. They choose to invest their lives in those needier than themselves to help make those lives better. They choose the worst possible environment believing they can do the most good with the people who have the least. I admire that. There is something very Christlike about that perspective and their pursuit. If you're like me, you admire people who care for the hurting and seek to provide help to the hopeless.

I'm convinced, as I read the life of Christ, that he wants us to emulate his concern for others. As he did, so he wants me to do also. Similar to him, we should be willing to show compassion to the needy by providing practical help. How should I? What does it look like at a level with which I can identify?

I also admire Norm Miller. He's the one who silently but powerfully organized the board and invested the money that has enabled the World Impact staff to serve and help so many in south Dallas. I was privileged to be present that day of conception when Norm, Ford Madison, Dr. Marvin Watson and Keith Phillips discussed the need for inner-city work in Dallas. Their heart concern was that the poor and disenfranchised might be offered help and hope by concerned Christian people. They discussed and I listened. We prayed and for six years nothing happened. Norm and I would talk about the dream. He and I, in our respective ways, would do what we could in prayer, but for so long no real solution was evident. Then four years ago, after years of petitions, the first couple stepped forward with the commitment to move full-time into the inner city. The Castons, like many of Keith's staff, gave up the American dream they were living—a life of education, prosperity and upward mobility—to serve a greater dream. They wanted to eternally impact the people of the inner city of Dallas.

Things haven't been the same since. Houses have been restored. A church has been formed. Kids have been instructed in the Bible. Single moms have been helped, and that whole neighborhood has a witness to the fact that God loves them. God is still in the reclamation business. And this section of south Dallas has seen evidence in its people, who have been rescued spiritually and practically, and in the community, which is slowly but perceptively being transformed. And I'm proud of them. They inspire me.

Where does such selfless character come from? What would motivate a successful, upwardly mobile couple to risk their own comfort and advancement for people with so little to offer in return? Why sacrifice for strangers who may reject them and who have already been overlooked and bypassed by society anyway? The answer again is Jesus. His life and ministry was centered on helping the helpless, not just spiritually, as we discussed in chapter one, but practically as we shall see next. Christ came to accomplish at least three things: (1) to redeem a spiritually incarcerated humanity; (2) to present in person his right and authority to rule all creation as the king of God's kingdom; and (3) to show demonstrably the kind intention of the heavenly Father.

Remember that God created us sinless and placed us in an environmental paradise. He loves us and wants us to enjoy the best of himself and the gifts he gives. But all of that was distorted and corrupted by humanity's original sin. Now perfection and paradise won't arrive until we are reunited with God in heaven. But between now and then, God's love remains constant. His compassion is limitless.

And Jesus demonstrated both God's compassionate concern and practical power by helping the helpless. Sometimes he fed them; sometimes he brought them back to life or calmed a storm or cast out a demon; sometimes he healed a seriously sick individual. That's where we find ourselves now. In this next passage we are confronted with two accounts of healing and their practical implications as lessons for us. As you read the account in Luke 5:12-26, notice the details, for they provide five important applications for the Master's men today.

> While Jesus was in one of the towns, a man came along who was covered with leprosy. When he saw Jesus, he fell with his face to the ground and begged him, "Lord, if you are willing, you can make me clean."
>
> Jesus reached out his hand and touched the man. "I am willing," he said. "Be clean!" And immediately the leprosy left him.
>
> Then Jesus ordered him, "Don't tell anyone, but go, show yourself to the priest and offer the sacrifices that Moses commanded for your cleansing, as a testimony to them."
>
> Yet the news about him spread all the more, so that crowds of people came to hear him and to be healed of their sicknesses. But Jesus often withdrew to lonely places and prayed.
>
> One day as he was teaching, Pharisees and teachers of the law, who had come from every village of Galilee and from Judea and Jerusalem, were sitting there. And the power of the Lord was present for him to heal the sick. Some men came carrying a paralytic on a mat and tried to take him into the house to lay him before Jesus. When they could not find a way to do this because

of the crowd, they went up on the roof and lowered him on his mat through the tiles into the middle of the crowd, right in front of Jesus.

When Jesus saw their faith, he said, "Friend, your sins are forgiven."

The Pharisees and the teachers of the law began thinking to themselves, "Who is this fellow who speaks blasphemy? Who can forgive sins but God alone?"

Jesus knew what they were thinking and asked, "Why are you thinking these things in your hearts? Which is easier: to say, 'Your sins are forgiven,' or to say, 'Get up and walk'? But that you may know that the Son of Man has authority on earth to forgive sins. . . ." He said to the paralyzed man, "I tell you, get up, take your mat and go home." Immediately he stood up in front of them, took what he had been lying on and went home praising God. Everyone was amazed and gave praise to God. They were filled with awe and said, "We have seen remarkable things today." (Luke 5:12-26)

In the first account Luke brings us face to face with a man with leprosy. Leprosy was the most dreaded disease of the ancient world. Lepers were thought to be highly contagious and incurable. As a result, their disease brought total social isolation and stigma. It is reminiscent of the AIDS epidemic today. Furthermore, the Mosaic law prohibited an infected person from associating with a noninfected person,[1] the practical outcome of which meant, to a Jew, dismissal from worship at the temple and estrangement from fellowship with other Israelites. The isolation and loneliness it engendered must have been a fate worse than death. Can you imagine having to hide from people though surrounded by them and having to alert any person within a few feet of you that you were a leper? I am sure that people walked around them, ran from them, didn't give them any eye contact or even a salutation. It must have been a demeaning, demoralizing existence. So I'm impressed when I see the way Jesus handled the situation.

Notice first that the encounter took place in a city. Cities are filled with people, so many, in fact, that it's easy to get lost in the crowd. It's hard to get personal in the city. The volumes of people tend to make people less friendly, more suspicious and harder to know.

I remember growing up in the Los Angeles area, a metropolis of over seven million people. In those kinds of cramped conditions people tend to be very protective of their space. At least it certainly seemed that way to me. There were so many people that to acknowledge them at times felt claustrophobic. It was easier to pretend that they weren't there, particularly if they were unattractive or had a problem or need—but not when Jesus came to town. When he arrived in this particular city, he noticed individuals and not just the beautiful or important citizens. He took note of a total outcast, someone like the forgotten residents of the wrong side of your city.

Second, notice that the critical issue the leper addressed was not Christ's ability. He apparently had heard enough of this messenger of God to know that Jesus had the power to heal, but he desperately wanted to know if Jesus would be *willing* to heal.

So it is with most of us. The issue in this illustration of copying our Master isn't whether we should help helpless people. I think the question is whether we'll take enough time to notice them. Are we so self-absorbed that we have neither time nor interest outside of our personal environment and personal agenda? Or do we have enough compassion to take the time to see a vagrant, recognize the needs of a fatherless boy or consider that the homeless might be cold this January? If we do, then we must answer another question: Are we willing to help?

We all have at least some ability to help, but will we? Now wait. I'm not talking about quitting your job and moving into the inner city like the Castons. But I am talking about what's right for you or me. What I see Jesus doing here is helping others according to the time, resources and ability he had. No more, but also, no less. You and I can do that too.

One of the small things my family has done through the years has been to create a sort of unofficial boy's ministry. I have three sons, and we love to camp, fish, play basketball or do whatever we can outdoors. Most boys do. I have noticed through the years that there were a lot of fatherless boys in my neighborhood. Most of the neighborhood boys had dads, but a lot of the dads were inattentive. Also, several of the boys were living alone with their mothers. So either way it seemed we had a constant army of boys playing football in the front yard or basketball in the backyard, and most would jump at the chance to go camping. So you know what we did? We took them on. Without formalizing a Boy Scout troop we ended up with something similar. And you can imagine the conversations we had with these kids after a pickup game or during a camping trip. God gave me many wonderful opportunities to counsel kids, take them to church, tell them about Jesus and sometimes simply be an encourager—in other words, act like a dad. It wasn't much. It didn't take a lot of extra energy, just the willingness to be inconvenienced from time to time with the extra head count in the house, at our dinner table or in our yard. But wow, did we get to see some lives changed as we saw one young man after another begin to follow the Master too.

Notice another small but significant observation from this text. One thing Jesus did that we can do too is add a personal touch. He actually touched the leper, an unheard of practice in his day. And don't you know it must've meant the world to that lonely, forgotten victim of such a dreaded disease. Sometimes hurting people will do better just by knowing someone cares. A conversation at work with a depressed coworker can make the difference in him continuing another day as well as believing that there might be hope for his life after all.

Helping doesn't have to take a lot of time. Sometimes it takes no more effort than sending a note to a hurting friend, but it can be a catalyst to them for emotional healing. We can do that kind of ministry, and when we do, our world will be better off for our effort.

Notice, fourth, that Jesus wanted no credit for his gift, but he did want God to get the glory. So he sent the healed man, armed with an incredible testimony, to the religious authorities. Surely they would be shocked to see him, recognizing that a miracle had taken place that day. And our Lord didn't bathe in notoriety. As quickly as the event concluded, Jesus stole away to refresh himself for the next opportunity of ministry. He apparently didn't need a plaque to commemorate his gift.

The next account is a companion to the first. Here Jesus is the focus of attention, not a leper. The group is composed of the esteemed religious and theological community. These professionals are convening in a home, not the city streets. And the helpless can't get to him because of the barrier of wall to wall inquisitors that surround our Master. But wait, several buddies conceive a daring plan to get their invalid friend in front of Jesus. Surely if they can just get the infirmed before the Master, Christ will heal him as he does others. How to do it? Well, since they can't get through the front door, why not tear the roof off of the host's house and lower their friend into the company of Jesus by ropes? I don't know who was more amazed: the owner of the home as he viewed the gaping hole in his roof or Jesus as he witnessed their audacious faith. But it doesn't matter, for the text only records the view of Jesus. This next statement, as recorded by Luke, reveals why good people who have horrible problems will try almost anything to get an audience with their Creator. Only God can help us when we face impossible circumstances, especially when the rest of humanity ignores us.

One of the reasons Christ came to the Israelites as their Messiah was to announce to them that he was their rightful king. They weren't expecting a heavenly ruler; they preferred a more normal, political and military-oriented liberator. Most Jews, though religious, were more concerned with the Roman occupation of their country then the spiritual residence of God in their hearts. They wanted a savvy Messiah who could rid them of Rome, not a spiritual Messiah requiring them to repent. So the credibility war was on. If the religious leaders could discredit Jesus, the crowd would quit following him, and they could once again turn their attention to exorcising that demon Caesar from their precious homeland. But, alas, it was not to be. Jesus was the real thing, the genuine fulfillment of all the ancient prophecies,[2] and he would not be stopped. So he brought the issue to the forefront by acting very Godlike. He dismissed the man's sins. Now any self-respecting religious authority would take issue with that, for no man could forgive sins except God alone. Why? First, because sin is primarily an affront to God, who is sinless and demands holiness. Second, sin also negatively affects other people. However, in the case of spiritual atonement (that is, the removal of the guilt of sin) only an act of God can confer such a pardon upon a guilty person.

So the Pharisees immediately took issue with him. However, our Lord's response was masterful. He decided to prove, with actions not words, that their accusation of blasphemy was false. Also, his actions would validate his deity and right to absolve the man of his sins. By reading their minds Christ was able to pose a penetrating question: "Which is easier, to forgive or heal?" Then, without waiting for an answer, he turned to the paralytic and commanded his healing and self-empowered departure—a true miracle for a paralytic.

The point was made dramatically and his deity proved conclusively. And, of course, the results were satisfying. A roomful of people was amazed as a helpless, hopeless person gave God glory.

The relevance of this passage provides the fifth and final critical application for a Master's man, which is the priority of addressing a person's spiritual need.

As a preface to this final application let me first sound this warning: beware the intimidation of your peers. You can be sure that when you set your course to help the forgotten of this world, some ignorant or arrogant or self-important souls will seek to change your course. Don't let them. If need be, be motivated by the overwhelming, even ridiculous, efforts the needy will try themselves in order to get help. We're not talking about fast-talking drifters who simply want your dollars for booze. I am talking about the sincere folk who will walk two hours before dawn to a minimum wage job because they don't have money for transportation. If they'll risk to find Christ, can't we risk to represent him?

Finally, don't miss the fact that Jesus raised the sin issue. No help is as lasting or meaningful as helping a person out of his bondage to sin. As with all of us, this begins and ends with a personal relationship with Jesus Christ. Drug treatment, therapy and other helps have their place for a hurting person, but a ministry of compassion that leaves out the gospel at best only provides a temporal benefit. Far better is the man who represents Jesus Christ and his redeeming grace as he provides practical help than those who don't. When I look to serve or for a place to give my money, I look for one that provides those two things. I seek ministry that holds the spiritual and practical in a healthy balance.

So what have we learned? What can we imitate? In summary, a Master's man first considers the helpless; second, demonstrates compassion in a personal way; third, gives help for God's glory not for our credit; and fourth, is a man, and not a wimp, not wishy-washy, but courageous and strong. You'll encounter critics when you try to show mercy. Don't let them intimidate you.

Fifth, a Master's man doesn't leave out the spiritual aspect. When helping others, when appropriate, share your faith. You may be the only one to take the time to do so. If presenting the gospel makes you nervous, walk them through the steps in chapter one. You can bet that if God has moved on your heart to help someone in difficult straits, he has probably worked on the person's heart to accept your help and to accept the one who has motivated you to do so—Jesus. He's the best friend a lonely, hurting person can have anyway.

7

CHANGE

Flexible Not Breakable

LUKE 5:27-39

*W*e are embarking on a new millennium. Not in our lifetime have the words "out with the old and in with the new" been more true. The decades beginning this new millennium will be marked by so many technological, social and geopolitical changes that we undoubtedly will be reconsidering totally how we live and relate to one another.

A *New York Times* editorial recently addressed the "coming age of biology" with the following thoughts: the hallmark of the twentieth century—from splitting the atom to cracking the genetic code—has been a faster advance over a wider range of activities than ever before in history. The chief questions now are whether science can continue its forward march or is losing momentum and whether its products will be harnessed for good or evil.

Jim Wright, former Speaker of the House, is concerned about issues related to the emergence of globalization. He warns,

"Globalization is an irreversible fact. Our challenge for the twenty-first century will be to control it, manage it and humanize it. There must be some common rules to assure that it serves rather than exploits ordinary people."[1]

The fact is that when it comes to change, some like it, some don't, and most wonder how best to deal successfully with the challenges it inevitably brings. We will all face change multiple times in our lives. Since that is true, the critical issue is the management of change, not resistance to it. The folks who are the most negatively influenced by change are those who seek to avoid it. They become calcified, if not broken altogether. The ones who succeed learn to use change for their benefit. They leverage change for an advantage either for themselves or others. It's never easy making friends from enemies, but I encourage you to do so as you face that familiar foe to the status quo—change. Jesus did, and I believe Luke 5:27-39 shows how enlightened he was and how tremendous the rewards are for following him.

Obviously change isn't easy. The longer and more successful you are at a certain thing, the harder it is to change. Not all change is good, but when change is precipitated by God, good will result. Sometimes the good that comes from change isn't easily recognizable until some time after the initial transition. When that is the case, the challenge of change is greater because we don't readily see the beneficial outcomes from our painful investment. And change involves pain because it usually is accompanied by loss. The loss can be any assortment of options—loss of the familiar, of security, of relationships, etc. Because change can be so costly and painful, it is important to weigh the risks and rewards, the costs and the benefits. Also, we should evaluate whether the change we are experiencing is due to a change of direction precipitated by God or whether we were the catalyst due to boredom, rebellion, pride, anger, greed or some other selfish factor. Being "content whatever the circumstances," as Paul recommends (Philippians 4:11), is a useful barometer in assessing the legitimacy of an opportunity to change. Sometimes change is demanded because of our diminished productivity, or it's necessitated by overwhelming evil, which you cannot stop. When these experiences are present, to change becomes your avenue to obedience and blessing or possibly your way of escape to insure your faithfulness.

What's important then is to assess each opportunity individually and measure its worth by God's purpose for your life. I recommend that you also evaluate its merits by testing it with Scripture, preceding it with prayer, seeking godly counsel from other Christians and considering any circumstantial evidence as well.

A friend of mine, Jeff Haddock, has shared a simple but helpful model for assessing your current position in the process of change and the next steps you will encounter as you move toward resolution and transformation. We all begin with a sense of denial when first confronted with significant change. And depending on our willingness to move forward to resolution, we will typically process the implications of the effects of change by analyzing the cause-and-effect relationship of the particular change to our circumstances. Jeff suggests that we tend to analyze cause and effect by reviewing four categories: our current focus, our needs, the opportunity before us and our responsibility in the midst of the challenge. According to Jeff, we will work through the four categories one by one. The speed will depend on a lot on personal as well as external factors, but I find that a chart like figure 7.1 helps me to see where on the change map I am at a given point of time, and that in itself provides some peace as well as some direction.

Denial	Commitment
Resistance	Exploration

Figure 7.1. Stages in the process of change

No matter how you process change, do not let fear control your decision-making process. In all things we must proceed by faith. Our faith must have as its object the Lord Jesus Christ. It must have as its basis the breadth of God's revelation. And it must align with our gifts, calling and temperament. Also, it will typically be an extension of our past history. Faith viewed in this way will never be capricious or presumptuous but will have the solid foundation of a godly perspective. Also, we will have peace, for we can rest in the assurance that the results are according to God's will, a will that glorifies Christ, meets our needs, provokes our growth and benefits others. That realization will help console the aching heart that grieves any loss that results from change. And it will provide courage to any soul, which must now begin to deal with a whole new pattern for living.

Change, as I've said, is a fact we can't avoid. We will all be faced with many different types of changes in our lifetime. For example, many men change jobs several times in a lifetime, and most will also make a complete career shift at least once.[2] Age, of course, dictates changes in our physical state. Our family life will go through many seasons of change as we marry, start a family, raise and launch children, bond again with our spouse in the empty nest, retire, etc. These things at minimum will happen in our families and may also include divorce, the death of a spouse or child, a life-debilitating disease or accident, or other traumatic events. The list may include moving, financial or economic change, health changes, as well as changes with friends, extended family and interests.

We might as well get used to the fact that things are going to change and develop a response that limits change's debilitating effects while capitalizing on its opportunities.

Is it easy? No, it's not. But Christ gives us a simple way of viewing change from a heavenly perspective while recognizing the challenges from an earthly vantage point.

Notice his view of the issue in Luke 5:27-39:

> After this, Jesus went out and saw a tax collector by the name of Levi sitting at his tax booth. "Follow me," Jesus said to him, and Levi got up, left everything and followed him.
>
> Then Levi held a great banquet for Jesus at his house, and a large crowd of tax collectors and others were eating with them. But the Pharisees and the teachers of the law who belonged to their sect complained to his disciples, "Why do you eat and drink with tax collectors and 'sinners'?"
>
> Jesus answered them, "It is not the healthy who need a doctor, but the sick. I have not come to call the righteous, but sinners to repentance."
>
> They said to him, "John's disciples often fast and pray, and so do the disciples of the Pharisees, but yours go on eating and drinking."
>
> Jesus answered, "Can you make the guests of the bridegroom fast while he is with them? But the time will come when the bridegroom will be taken from them; in those days they will fast."
>
> He told them this parable: "No one tears a patch from a new garment and sews it on an old one. If he does, he will have torn the new garment, and the patch from the new will not match the old. And no one pours new wine into old wineskins. If he does,

the new wine will burst the skins, the wine will run out and the wineskins will be ruined. No, new wine must be poured into new wineskins. And no one after drinking old wine wants the new, for he says, 'The old is better.' " (Luke 5:27-39)

"After this." After what? After he had showed them he had the authority to forgive sins. Then he showed he had the authority to ask people to follow him. Also, he showed he had the right to access previously forbidden places. And furthermore, he had the authority to waive the rules on fasting. Finally, he had the right to formulate a new process for reaching the lost.

I don't know about you, but when I finally get to the gate at the airport and sit down to wait for my plane, I am delighted if I see that someone has left the paper—especially the sports page. On occasion I've been left with only the middle section. The first page is critical in understanding the second half of the article. The first page sets the tone and establishes the main idea. It will also contain some pertinent information to which succeeding sentences will refer from the middle sections of the paper. That is exactly the predicament here.

When this section of Scripture opens with the phrase "after this," I feel that I'm in an airport looking at an incomplete sports page. I want to see the front page. I want to know what's going on and what critical information precedes this. What is "after this" referring to? In this section of Scripture the "after this" refers to the healing of the paralytic in the previous passage (Luke 5:17-26). Christ's power and authority were demonstrated to a group of skeptical religious leaders as he presented irrefutable proof that he was the Messiah, the Savior of the world. Jesus the Son of God never performed miracles indiscriminately. They were always purposeful, and the purpose was greater than the temporary relief from suffering that the mira-

cle resolved. Christ's miracles had the greater purpose of vali-
dating his message and identity as Son of God, Messiah and
Savior of the world. His message: "Repent, for the kingdom of
heaven is near" (Matthew 4:17). And so it was in the healing of
the paralytic. And in so doing he provided an irrefutable
answer to the religious leaders that he as God had the authority
(and power) to forgive sins—and to change unnecessarily
inhibiting traditions.

Luke wants the readers to carry that idea forward and into the
next section of Scripture. He wants us to see that Jesus also had
the power and authority (1) to call and command people to follow
him, (2) to go into previously ignored places in order to extend the
offer to repent and prepare for the kingdom, (3) to waive ineffective religious rituals such as fasting, and (4) to extend freedom to
his people to discover the most effective and creative means possible to invite people into a relationship with God.

The first challenge of change is evident in the calling of Levi
(also called Matthew in the other Gospel accounts) to be a disciple of Jesus. This challenge involves developing a relationship
with people with whom we would not normally associate. In
first-century Palestine there were separate cultures coexisting
but struggling to accept one another. One classic work
describes it this way: "There were two worlds in Jerusalem, side
by side. On the one hand, was Grecianism with its theater and
amphitheater; foreign tendencies and ways, from the foreign
King downwards. On the other hand, was the old Jewish world,
becoming now set and ossified in the Schools of Hillel and
Shammai, and overshadowed by Temple and Synagogue. And
each was pursuing its course, by the side of the other."[3] The
Jews with their scrupulous religious traditions, prejudices and
separatism lived in hated subjugation to the Romans who occu-
pied the land and flaunted their military power, paganism,

excesses and financial domination. The two sides tolerated each other out of necessity. The Jews had no choice, and the Romans didn't want to provoke an uprising that would necessitate fresh troops and military expenditures and draw the ire of Rome and Caesar. They hated each other, and just under the diplomatic surface of day-to-day existence boiled a cauldron of seething resentment by the Jews toward their foreign captors.

And in this world there was perhaps no person more hated by the Jewish community and no more ostracized than the tax collector. Not only did the Jews loathe paying him in order to fund the pagan emperor's occupation of their homeland, they despised those Jewish traitors whom Rome paid to excise taxes from their own people. Levi was just such a Jewish traitor. Also, it is well documented that the tax collectors got rich by over-collecting from their countrymen.

In Christ's invitation to Levi to follow him, I see a principle in the text concerning God's offer of grace to imperfect people. As usual, God looks at our hearts, not our professional profiles or our histories filled with mistakes and regrets. He looks only at our willingness to repent from old ways and redirect our steps toward him, where all things are new.[4] So, with Christ's invitation, Levi left his past and followed Christ toward a new beginning.

Our blessed God does the same thing today. Only God can take the professional and so alter his thinking that he radically changes the orientation of his profession. God can give a man a new purpose for living and working. He gives a noble reason for pursuing our life's work. He occasionally, as with Levi, will extricate us from a profession entirely, especially when its whole concept lacks integrity, by providing a more honest occupation. More often than not, however, he redirects the receptive person, enlarges our view of his purposes and infuses that intent into our livelihood. Suddenly we find a desire to use our job for God's glory, and we see our professional position as our platform for honoring Christ. Interestingly, any man who views his job as a ministry will soon see his clients and coworkers as objects of compassion as he desires for them the same liberating experience he enjoys in Christ.

Unfortunately, it's not unusual to catch a little flack from old friends when we change the intentionality of our work and relationships. But that's the challenge of change when we involve ourselves with people.

Closely linked to the change of relationships are change and the places we may now go. After our Lord graciously invited Levi to become one of the Master's team of followers, Levi enthusiastically invited Jesus over to his house to meet some friends. Now if Levi was an outcast, who do you think his friends were? That's right— social, economic and religious outcasts such as him. And did our Lord balk at the request? Of course not! The love of God precludes all prejudice, fear and defilement. So Christ went to the party and no doubt had a blast. You know it's always fun to be with Jesus. He doesn't have a puckered face, a soured attitude. He is fun-loving, free, creative and always drawing out the good in a thing. It must have been so inspiring to be with him. However, that was until the religious bigots showed up. Rigid and uptight, they condemned Christ for the company he kept. They wanted to know why he associated with such raw humanity. The answer was simple: God seeks those who have needs, and all who have needs are welcome to have a relationship with him. Of course, that points out a dilemma.

It seems that the only ones offended with Jesus and who thereby never receive the benefit of a relationship with God are those who think they're better than the more obviously needy people, those who think they're OK. What an irony and a shame. The Bible, the daily newspaper and human experience all point to the same universal sad fact. No one is perfectly OK.

We all have our dark areas. We all have sinned and come short of the perfection of God.[5] So, although all of us need a relationship with God and have been welcomed by God, the only ones who forgo the amazing change that God provides are the ones too snobbish to see their need.

I'm sure Christ's heart broke seeing the goody-goody people, the religious leaders, miss that simple truth, but he didn't let it stop him from carrying out his task of offering the world forgiveness and a new relationship with God.

Therefore, when the religious hardliners, meaning to intimidate him, threw another question at Jesus, he shot it down with yet another answer based on God's grace. Christ said, essentially, that when God changes a man he also changes the patterns of his life.

Let me explain. *Grace* means unmerited favor, in other words, a gift. It's free, the opposite of effort, works and compensation. The Jewish religious leaders believed that self-effort could win God's favor. They thought that if a man were religious enough, lived scrupulously by certain rules and traditions, then God would endorse his efforts, smile on his sacrifice and extend acceptance. However, that is not how God works and never has been. Though these strict students of the Old Testament Scripture had studied the trees (the fine points of the Bible), they had missed the forest (the overriding point of God's love). The Old Testament Scripture was thorough in its detail of the character of God—perfect, holy. It was transparent concerning man as well—flawed, apt to trouble. The message of the Old Testament—the commands to behave like God—was intended to show flawed humanity that no one could be good enough. It was an instructional process meant to lead people to the acknowledgment of their failure and a recognition of the fact they we all need God's favor. The Bible's intent is to motivate men and women to realize their need for a God who desires to give us a break and extend forgiveness.[6] Spread throughout the Old Testament was the message of hope for an exasperated searcher that God would forgive, accept and justify us if we would simply believe that he would.[7] He will free us from the penalty of sin and accept us fully forgiven. That's grace. Unmerited favor. That's what God would give—forgiveness—though we don't deserve it. In fact, God gives grace in spite of the fact we don't deserve it.

So when the religious leaders questioned Christ's lack of adherence to the grueling religious ritual of fasting, through simple language Jesus proclaimed that God intends for his people to celebrate his grace and not to strenuously attempt to earn it.

The bridegroom in this passage refers to Christ, the one who brought the realization of God's free gift of forgiveness to humankind. The guests of the bridegroom are those of us who are associated with him. We get to enjoy his company and ignore unnecessary religious rituals because we have a real, not ritual, relationship with God. There is no need to seek another method of winning God's favor. Christ's coming to earth meant a whole new thing was happening. And with a whole new thing there came a whole new process or pattern for drawing people to God. God used the Old Testament law given to the Jews and administered by the Jewish religious system to demonstrate their need for God through the reminder of personal failure that breaking God's law would bring. Through Christ, though, God was inaugurating a whole new way of getting humankind's attention. God would draw people's interest to himself by revealing his infinite love, forgiveness and acceptance through his Son. Jesus was such an attractive alternative to the demands and consequent failures of a strict code of religious legalism that people flocked to him. They did then, and they do now.

But we struggle with this. We struggle with change involving people with whom we wouldn't normally associate, places we wouldn't normally go and patterns we wouldn't ordinarily employ. We struggle with people because people can hurt our reputation, our sense of status. We're concerned about our social group and how it enhances our reputation and reflects on our sense of dignity and self-worth. We're very concerned about the places we go because places can make us insecure and uncomfortable. We prefer safety and security. We like the elevation and status of going to the best places and attaining the highest positions.

And new patterns interrupt our sense of direction and meaning. We've spent a lifetime developing a certain way of life and a means to support that lifestyle. But to associate with people that society looks down at, to go places society typically bypasses, to do things that are abnormal and against the flow of successful people, that's a challenge and perhaps something that Christ would change in us. Think back to that great change God made in you—if you have been through the new birth in Jesus. Aren't you glad that he extricated you from some of the relationships you were in, the places you went, the things you did? Don't you think he would want you occasionally to go and retrieve some needy individual who's caught in the web of self-destruction? You might be his emissary with the message of hope to some soul-searching person. Do you realize that you are the Master's ambassador?[8]

Perhaps it's wise to consider as you grow and mature in Christ that there may yet need to be some changes in you. Does there need to be a change in whom you hang out with, where you go, how you do things? Perhaps there's some room for improvement, and that's a challenge of change.

This passage gives us permission to change the way we enjoy

our relationship with God and should cause us to change how we relate to people. We too should seek to attract people to God by reflecting God's openness and not our harshness.

So the first concepts of the Master's direction were new people, new places and new patterns. Now our Lord caps off his presentation on change with a parable. Using two very common illustrations from his era, our Master instructs us that new times necessitate new methods, materials and manners. Jesus reminds his hearers that just as new cloth cannot patch an old garment for fear of tearing it, neither can a person fill an old wine container with new wine without the container expanding and cracking, allowing all the contents to be spilled out. New things must be accompanied by new approaches that are better able to accommodate the change. Unfortunately, the problem of rigidity isn't confined to the first century; it's present in the church today. As one author has suggested, "Protestantism is caught in a stifling web of institutionalism. The wineskins have grown rigid and it is not enough to call for change or proclaim the need. The whole problem of wine skins, the structure of the church, must be dealt with."[9]

Certainly the church is challenged to adapt to an ever-changing world without adopting the world's perspective.

But what about you? What is new for you? Is your faith new? Are you a new believer in Christ? If so, then look for new friends to hang out with without totally dismissing your contacts with your old friends, the people whom Christ would like to meet next. However, it is imperative that you associate with people who share your new values and will support you in learning to reorient your life to the new direction that you been given in Christ.[10] You probably need to establish some new priorities such as regular prayer, Bible study and community worship. You may need some new habits, breaking off the old, such as how you live, work and recreate, but not to the exclusion of ignoring your old friends. Christ may want you to be the magnet that draws that whole group to him. And that will take some creativity.

Perhaps you are a longtime member of the fraternity of Jesus but are in a new season of life. Maybe something has changed in your job, community, family or health. How will you respond? With the same old methods? This passage reminds us that new times necessitates new methods. Raising teenagers, for example, will take methods different from those you used to raise toddlers. Communicating with business clients today is very different from the days before websites, the Internet, faxes, mobile phones and pagers. And it will probably change some more. Are you ready?

Marriage after twenty-five years takes some fresh thinking. If you are going to grow more vibrant, romantic and close, you can't do at twenty-five years what you did at five years. Remain, yes, but not grow.

So beware: the better you are today at what you do, the greater the challenge will be tomorrow to transition into something new. The longer you do something, the more insecure you can become with the prospect of changing it.[11] As one authority on change has asserted, "It takes an effort to perceive in the enemy one's own best opportunity"—the enemy being change. Our Lord understands that. That's why he said that old people doing the same old thing think it is good enough. That's why I believe God guided Luke to insert this section of Scripture into his Gospel. Here our Master recognizes change, celebrates its opportunities, sees its inevitability and, in so doing, prepares us for confronting it successfully. I appreciate that because I have learned that change is constant and relentless. Change will be the environment of the new millennium. I need to be ready, I need to be nimble, and I need to trust Christ to guide me. Ready or not, here it comes; change is rapidly upon us.

8

RIGIDITY

Rules Without Love

LUKE 6:1-11

What a lousy way to end a great day. It was opening day of duck season 1997. My sons and I had just finished one of the most productive hunts ever. Then as I was bending over picking up decoys, I saw him. Right out into the water he marched, and the next thing I knew, this straight-faced, no-nonsense game warden was going through my credentials, questioning me on every aspect of our hunt and then probing through my shotgun shell satchel. *Oops,* he found something. There it was, some left over dove load from dove season that I had failed to remove from my hunting pouch. You can use lead shot for dove, but a few years ago the government changed the law on migratory waterfowl and mandated steel shot. I was in violation of the law.

As if the goof-up wasn't bad enough, now I got the grilling. First he stated the violation, quoting the law, and then began to issue the citation. Then it got worse; he asked what my profession was. Oh how I wished at that moment to be a salesman or fireman or doctor or something—anything but a minister. But armed with that information, he launched into a humiliating sermon on his disappointment with me, "the minister." He went on to tell me of his personal spiritual status and the expectations of the church he attended. Furthermore, he stated rather demeaningly how I was so wide of the mark. It was all I could do to hold my attitude and say, "Yes sir." To add insult to injury, I later found out from my oldest son that the warden had mentioned what a poor father I was and the shameful example I was setting—as if he knew anything about my family or me! I wanted to punch him and earn my reputation. Fortunately, he was long gone by then, and I was left shamed and sorry.

You need to understand that I grew up duck hunting. Through the years I've seen bag limits fluctuate, laws change regarding the permissibility of certain types of firearms, and a myriad of other evolutionary legislative issues affecting this sport, and I've never been ticketed. Fortunately, I've not only kept up with the changing laws but remembered to change shells, put the choke in my gun, not shoot female mallards and so forth. But this time I slipped up, and the man assigned to uphold the law was there to enforce it and expose my violation. OK, OK, I had it coming, but I didn't expect the ridicule and condemnation, nor do I think that it was professional or necessary. But the fact is I got both barrels from a verbally vindictive warden, and I felt a lot smaller for the encounter.

Ever been there yourself? How about with other Christians? Sometimes the most legalistic and condemning people we encounter are those who follow that forgiving role model—Jesus Christ.

It doesn't take being in the Christian faith long before you run into somebody who's all too willing to point out your mishaps. They are the "hey, you shouldn't be doing that" police. Typically, that first time of confrontation causes you to back up a step, intimidated, unsure of yourself, ashamed that knowingly or unknowingly you somehow blew it, defacing the reputation of religion and somehow casting a shadow on the character of God himself. Most of us stop the act immediately to review the situation and figure out what it was that we did wrong. What commandment or other Christian principle did we just violate?

However, for those who have been in the faith for a while, you soon discover that the rules of behavior codified by the Christian community often have nothing to do with the character of God, which is what God's law was originally meant to reflect and protect. The passage that we're about to look at in Luke 6:1-11 gives us a primary example of that fact. Many of the rules and regulations that become entrenched as traditions in the Christian community often don't reflect accurately the character of God[1] or "the kind intention of His will."[2]

What are we to do? Who can unravel the confusion of what rules to obey? Fortunately we have an answer and example in chapter 6 of Luke. In this passage we will see Jesus stand up to the legalists of his day by demonstrating love. He will confidently manifest that especially attractive characteristic of compassion despite significant opposition. He exemplifies for us a compassion that cares for the needs of the individual, not for the security of a bureaucracy, a mercy that pities the needy while demonstrating a courage that boldly stands up to the insecurity of the people who feel a need to be in control. And control, in the final analysis, is the seedbed of legalism.

Legalism flourishes in systems governed by people who find security in being in charge—totally and without challenge. The root of the problem, I believe, is that the legalists are carrying a lot of anxiety, even paranoia, that says that "if it's not done this way—my way—the whole system will collapse." What a shame they haven't learned the fundamental truth that they can release their human anxieties to the one in heaven who controls all things and allows us to be under his control through the power of the Holy Spirit. That's a vertical relationship based on faith, but legalists don't understand faith. They only know rules.

One dictionary defines legalism as "strict, often too strict, law or adherence to a code. Theologically, the doctrine of salvation by good works."[3] But we Christians know that salvation is by grace through faith. In other words, our relationship with God is established because he chose to accept us despite our unworthiness, and we believed that he would and took him up on his offer. It is a gift of God. But we stumble regularly over that simple principle, believing that somehow we earn the favor of God by behavioral adherence through a code of righteous conduct or at least can maintain the relationship by rigid obedience to a list of predetermined, culturally entrenched rules. And these same misguided folks are all too ready to jump on your case if ever you are caught not toeing their line. How unfortunate. How divisive and counterproductive. How estranged from truth and grace. The apostle Paul, author of most of the New Testament, is quite clear in stating God's perspective on religious law. He tells us that the law was intended only to be as a schoolmaster, to teach us that we needed mercy and grace so that we would be inclined to migrate to Christ.[4]

The problem with legalism is that it steals the joy from faith.

It creates fear as it seeks to control through intimidation. As a result, it affects how you take care of yourself (as we shall see in verses 1-5), and it can affect how you take care of others (verses 6-11). Personally, I believe it all begins with a misunderstanding of what is sacred. Once our focus is redirected to the wrong *sacred,* there is a steady proliferation of the ridiculous, which stifles creativity, limits liberty and squelches joy. And all of this eventually threatens our spiritual health.

Chuck Swindoll has written eloquently on this subject, and his words express my feelings. I appreciate the following quote from his book *The Grace Awakening*:

> Too many folks are being turned off by a twisted concept of the Christian life instead of offering a winsome and contagious, sensible, and achievable invitation of hope and cheer through the sheer power of Christ. More people than ever are projecting a grim face character of religion on demand. I find it tragic that religious killjoys have almost taken the freedom and fun out of faith. People need to know that there is more to the Christian life than deep frowns, pointing fingers, and unrealistic expectations. Harassment has had the floor long enough.[5]

Let's see if that isn't true as we review the two accounts Luke has recorded on the subject. In both accounts one theme is prominent: the question of the sabbath.

> One Sabbath Jesus was going through the grainfields, and his disciples began to pick some heads of grain, rub them in their hands and eat the kernels. Some of the Pharisees asked, "Why are you doing what is unlawful on the Sabbath?"
>
> Jesus answered them, "Have you never read what David did when he and his companions were hungry? He entered the house of God, and taking the consecrated bread, he ate what is lawful only for priests to eat. And he also gave some to his com-

panions." Then Jesus said to them, "The Son of Man is Lord of the Sabbath."

On another Sabbath he went into the synagogue and was teaching, and a man was there whose right hand was shriveled. The Pharisees and the teachers of the law were looking for a reason to accuse Jesus, so they watched him closely to see if he would heal on the Sabbath. But Jesus knew what they were thinking and said to the man with the shriveled hand, "Get up and stand in front of everyone." So he got up and stood there.

Then Jesus said to them, "I ask you, which is lawful on the Sabbath: to do good or to do evil, to save life or to destroy it?"

He looked around at them all, and then said to the man, "Stretch out your hand." He did so, and his hand was completely restored. But they were furious and began to discuss with one another what they might do to Jesus. (Luke 6:1-11)

The issue facing the Jewish community in Jesus' time was whether the sabbath was sacred. That is, was keeping the sabbath an inviolable principle to which all other issues were subordinate? The Pharisees, a religious sect of legalists or regulationalists, were convinced that it and all the supporting traditions that surrounded the sabbath were. But Christ thought otherwise. So what's the big deal?

Sabbath (Hebrew *shabat*) literally means "repose, cessation from exertion." God initiated it when he "rested" from the work of creation.[6] But it was not universally recognized until it was instituted by Moses through the Ten Commandments, which are the core of the Mosaic law. The purpose of the sabbath was to give the people of God a rest from their continuous labor, which was a result of the Fall—the consequence of their original sin. God's perfect work was completed in six days, so he rested on the seventh. Man's work will not be completed until we are reunited with God in his heavenly kingdom through

Christ, but the sabbath was given so that we would have a reminder of this hope. Therefore, we are to set aside (sanctify) a day in honor of this great hope in honor of God. In that sense, he made it holy, special, without corruption, a beautiful symbol of a reality yet to come.

Merrill Unger in his classic work *Unger's Bible Dictionary* tells us that the Jewish observance was indeed a

> strict cessation of labor. . . . Moses wrote for example that there could be no gathering of kindling for cooking, no burden bearing, traveling or trading in the market. There was to be a celebration of worship. It was to be a day of gladness.[7]

The object, according to Unger, of the cessation and community worship was to give humans

> the opportunity to engage in such mental and spiritual exercises as would tend to the quickening of soul and spirit and the strengthening of the spiritual life. In the highest sense, the Sabbath was made for man's spiritual enjoyment and development.[8]

However, it wasn't long until all of this was twisted into such an elaborate series of specific regulations that one could hardly leave the house without breaking the sabbath.

In my library I am fortunate to have several commentaries on books of the Bible. These commentaries, hundreds of pages long on any one book of the Bible, are an exhaustive human explanation of the plain text of Scripture. Can you imagine trying to regulate your Christian life based on the compilation of all these authors' commentaries on the fine points of the Bible? It's overwhelming. It's impossible. Don't you find it hard enough just to read your Bible and apply it to your life in simple terms, much less the writings of this scholar or that theologian? It's way too confusing, and so it was in the first century.

In fact, the first-century Jews were told that activities such as picking heads of grain and rubbing them in their hands to eat was the same as reaping and threshing and were thereby acts of labor and prohibited. Jews were allowed to walk only so many paces from the home, or it was considered traveling. And so it went. It was a burdensome, cumbersome, social-religious environment into which the Lord of grace stepped that Saturday morning.

In the first case study on legalism we see Jesus and his men walking through a wheat field, taking a few heads of grain and eating them in order to satisfy their hunger. The Pharisees were upset with this and confronted Jesus about his violation of the rules. I'm impressed with the way Christ handled this. If it had been me, I would've turned these legalists back to the law to show them that in Exodus 12:16 it was permissible to prepare whatever food whatever way was necessary for the day's nourishment. Also it was permissible, according to a passage found in Deuteronomy 23:24-25, to pick fruits or vegetables from a garden in order to nourish oneself. So, in fact, our Lord wasn't breaking the law, but he was breaking the code of behavior that the religionists had developed. However, Christ didn't use that tactic. Instead, he went back to a fairly obscure section of Scripture in the life of David that pointed out that David was allowed to "break the law" to eat bread ordinarily set aside for the priests alone to eat. David was permitted this leniency because his men and he were starving as they ran from a vindictive, insane king who had issued a death warrant for their lives. This allowance for David extended by the priests and condoned by God gave evidence to the fact that God's character is represented in the various symbols that we use in our religious observances. They are meant to show his holiness but also his overwhelming concern for our welfare because he loves us.

Religious symbols are intended to be instructive, not restrictive.

God's original law was intended for our benefit, not for our harm. It was to give us the liberty to know God and to enjoy a relationship with him, not to confine our quest to know God. The sabbath was a God-ordained rest for the welfare of humans, who need refreshment from our persistent labors.

When Jesus declared that he was Lord of the sabbath, he was telling the legalists that he had the authority to interpret Scripture. His commentary on what was permissible within the intent of God's concern for the welfare of humanity was the final word on the subject. And aren't we glad? Jesus commented that David's use of the consecrated bread was permissible in the spirit of the sabbath, for its nourishment relieved their burden of hunger just as a day off relieves the burden of labor.

These Pharisees had missed the point of the law, which is meant to insure the health and welfare of humanity from the toils incurred by the curse. The law had become an end in and of itself and therefore a new curse. Our Lord tried graciously to point this out to these hardheaded spiritual leaders of Israel by retelling the anecdote of David. Unfortunately, the rabbis weren't satisfied. They held tenaciously to the letter of the law, so another confrontation ensued. And this one would revolve around healing.

As the lens of understanding focuses on our next case study, we see our Lord entertained in worship in a synagogue. He is reading the Scripture when in walks a handicapped man. The legalists were watching closely to see if he would dare heal a man on the sabbath, because their law expressly forbade medical exercises as another form of work. They were perched in their snobbery, ready to pounce on him with yet another condemnation. The Master read their minds (which should have been proof enough that he had the authority to modify their archaic standards) and, after having the man walk to the front of the synagogue, asked the crowd whether it was lawful to do good or evil on the sabbath. Jesus asked them if the sabbath was for saving lives or destroying them. What a great question to highlight the purpose of God's instituted holy days.

Without waiting for an answer, our Lord healed the man, thereby substantiating God's loving intent for humankind. His law was intended for the benefit of you and me. The Master's healing proved that. Healing relieves the burden of affliction just as a day off allows the sores and aches of labor a time to heal. That was the interpretation Jesus wanted the Jews to recognize, but they were blinded by their rules. Unfortunately, the Pharisees of Jesus' day missed the point again—as do today's Pharisees. It is sad but true that these types of people value control as an antidote to their insecurities rather than grace through faith.

On behalf of the first-century Jews I will say that some of their paranoia was well founded. Their insecurities sprang from their failure as a nation to worship God exclusive of all other forms of worship. What began as a national movement to maintain the moral conscience of their nation ultimately led to the ridiculous rigidity of Jesus' day. Those Jewish ancestors had experienced the most heinous agony of persecution through their exile in Babylon from the years 605 through 445 B.C. They vowed never to fall prey to spiritual infidelity again. And so to protect their community from the pagan influences of culture and to provide for the stability of their spiritual life, they developed a lengthy code known as the Talmud. But by Jesus' day the code had become so focused on the life of a pious Jew that the singular test by which a man or woman could feel accepted in the community was compliance with the religious rules of Judaism. The cost of all of this containment was a stifling, lifeless, joyless religious existence. Jesus sought to dismantle that straightjacket then, and he still does today.

So what good are religious symbols anyway? I believe that worship symbols are meant to encourage godliness. Unfortunately, symbols can eventually be viewed as the means of godliness. In some Christian traditions the sacraments—baptism and the Lord's Supper or Eucharist—which are intended to reflect the grace that has already been given to the believer, are instead twisted to become the provision of grace. Instead of being a visual celebration of the invisible endowment of God's love to an individual person of faith, they become a benchmark. We find ourselves striving and sometimes straining to qualify for these graces. Some people, for instance, rigorously attend mass or other services and dutifully pursue the catechisms in order to reach a level of compliance whereby the religious authorities will then acknowledge the conferral of grace and, so to speak, allow them to join the club.

Conversely, for others, the legalistic traditions have developed systems whereby if a person behaves in a certain way, he or she will be deemed unworthy of fellowship and may even have his or her personal relationship with God questioned. Behavior outside these strict codes verifies, for the new legalist, that God's grace is not at work in your life. Dancing is excluded, drinking is excluded, and special days are to be remembered scrupulously. Special activities are to be performed. Entertainment may be excluded, and other parts of culture are deemed unholy or undesirable.

But I have a question: Who says so? I prefer we take a minute to think for ourselves and then ask ourselves the question: Why do we do what we do?

If what you do behaviorally is the way in which you help others to know Christ, or if what you do is the way in which you develop your relationship with Christ, it seems to me that this is your business. I firmly believe that the question of whether you should or should not (on an issue that is not addressed in Scripture) is a matter between you and God and, of course, your wife who has to live with you. Therefore, if you can justify your behavior before God, who am I to tell you differently? If you want to experience God's freedom on a particular issue,[9] then I suggest you process the issue through the following screen. First, make sure that the issue is truly optional and does not conflict with Scripture, including those passages that tell us to take into consideration how our behavior influences others,[10] then take the next step. Second, seek the counsel of your spouse and trustworthy fellow Christians. Third, make certain your intent is not rebellious but truly for the building up of other people that they may know God too. Finally, having prayed and sensing God's peace, have at it.

The issue isn't whether or not my means in knowing Christ and making him known should be your means. The point of this passage is that religious rules are meant to focus on a religious leader—Jesus our Savior. They are not to be an end unto themselves. And religious days are meant to be a benefit to God's people. God's reprieve is for our improvement, not for our social or religious acceptance by others.

Alexander Solzhenitsyn, seeing the dangers of a legalistic society, has helped us in writing:

> The society based on the letter of the law and never reaching any higher fails to take advantage of the full range of human possibilities. The letter of the law is too cold and formal to have a beneficial influence on society. Whenever the tissue of life is woven of legalistic relationships this creates an atmosphere of spiritual mediocrity that paralyzes man's noblest impulses.[11]

Isn't that good? It takes thoughtful initiative to ask ourselves what God wants us to do rather than let someone else do our thinking for us. It takes self-discipline to spend time in Scripture, pray and meditate to discover the mind of God and know the person of God rather than mindlessly and heartlessly leaning on the repetitious religious mantra of some brand of legalism. It takes creativity and nobility to walk into an arena of our secularized culture and determine how best to walk as Jesus walked, how to reflect unapologetically his love and grace to others. It takes a Master's type of man to extend courageously his forgiveness, to invite the sinner to know Christ as you've known him, without erecting any unnecessary barriers.

But beware, there are plenty of opponents to this way of thinking. People are often suspicious and competitive. Their insecurities cause them to seek uniformity before allowing individuality. Ultimately it's a desire to control. In the desire to control outcomes we try to control processes. And in the desire to control processes we end up controlling people—the very people Christ said he came to set free.[12]

The characteristics of opposition are *conformity,* which frowns on individuality; *rejection,* which breeds isolation; *division,* which destroys fellowship; *rigidity,* which tends to stifle creativity; and *condemnation,* which leaves everyone but the control artist feeling guilty. In this system everything is painted the same color and no one is allowed to paint outside the lines.

But our Lord is boundless in his patience, not wanting any to miss his grace but wanting all to enjoy his company. So he tolerates our petty systems while calling us to a life of unbridled faith. Sure enough, there is only one way to heaven, through Jesus Christ our Lord. But there are many ways to express our love and affection toward him and to express his love to others in our world. Beware of adopting somebody else's policies;

beware of pushing your policies on others as well.

But what are the cures for legalism?

First and foremost, I would say love. Loving God with all your heart, mind, soul and strength will enable you to love others as you love yourself and to do that which is best for them rather that what's best for you. Love will enable you to allow others the flexibility they need to grow in their relationship with God, even to allow people to make their own mistakes without condemning and rejecting. Love helps us acknowledge that God is God, and we are not his deputies in judging others.

As you move through life and encounter competitive opposition in the religious realm, allow me to offer some advice. First, recognize the philosophy behind it. Does it make sense? Is it logical? Is it possible that your opponent is right? This is a matter for personal reflection and review. I'm not condoning libertinism. I'm not saying that anything goes in the Christian faith once we know Christ. That's why it's important to watch what others are doing and saying to see if some of it does apply to us. But don't be bound by it just because they say it. Use your head. Ask God what's best for you.

Second, review your position and motive. Make sure your heart is right and that the principles you're standing on will biblically hold the weight of your conviction and effort. What does the Bible say about this situation? What does it not say? Perhaps the Bible's silence allows you a measure of freedom that others haven't seen. If so, then, third, respond appropriately. To those who really disagree and don't understand what you're doing, to the degree that you can, discuss the matter, reason with them. Some condemning legalists need a time of conversation and clarification. On the other hand, some need confrontation. They need to be told they have no business sticking their bony finger in your chest. Remember that legalism has a tendency to grow, and the only way that we can stop the intimidation is by standing strong. Biblical confrontation (that is, speaking the truth in love) is a step we must sometimes take. And remember too that no one needs retaliation. In the final analysis, let it go if you can't get agreement with your condemner. Let him go his way and you go yours. Finally, remain on course. If you're doing the right things for the right reasons, go forward. Catching flak is just part of being a difference-maker in Christ. As men who seek to know Christ and make him known, we should not be surprised by the fact that our world will misunderstand us. Even our fellow Christians will often look down on us. Don't be surprised by the conflict. Don't be surprised by institutionalized legalism and its impediments, which stifle the growth of the church and challenge your enthusiasm for grace. Expect it, expose it when appropriate, express the alternative that is available in Christ, and make sure to examine your own motives so that what you do is done in love and in the grace that God has shed on you and desires to share with others.[13]

It still galls me when I think of that game warden coming down on me so hard, which says something about how painful the effects of legalism are on us as well. And maybe that is why this subject is so important to me. I don't want to be a grace killer. I don't want to be a Christian condemner. I want to be like Jesus. I want to put grace on display. And I want that game warden to really enjoy his relationship with Christ too and not let all the lawbreakers steal his joy. Who knows, maybe he will read this book. I wish him well if he does, and I wish you well too. God bless you.

9

DECISIONS

Making the Majors Right

LUKE 6:12-19

---

*D*ecision-makers. They come in all shapes and sizes. Some are procrastinators: "Let's wait." There are those who make snap decisions: "Now." Some hands-off types: "You decide." Some butt it: "You know what you ought to do." Some analyze: "Let's weigh the pros and cons." I suppose all have their place, and all can be misused. But when push comes to shove, and it's time to make a pivotal decision, one that will change the status and direction of your future, I want to ask you a question: How do you go about making that pivotal decision? And are you aware enough of its implications to recognize that the issue is critical?

This is such an important topic because we are in a constant process of decision-making, and over a lifetime we will make several life-changing decisions. Where do we go to school? Whom do we marry? Plus we will deal with career direction, major purchases, lifestyle pursuits, etc. Also I'll bet, if we're honest, at this point in our lives we'd have to admit we've made our share of lousy decisions and have had to live with the consequences. I know I have. Haven't you?

I remember when I was sixteen and couldn't wait to have a car. I didn't have a whole heck of a lot of money, but I knew the car I wanted. An older kid from school drove a beautiful 1957 Chevy. It had black tuck-and-roll interior, and the outside was painted a glorious blue. He'd gone through it from headlight to taillight redoing and customizing the car; it was beautiful. Now don't get me wrong. I'm not that old. This wasn't 1958. But when I was in high school in the early seventies, that '57 was one sharp, classic car to own. When the day came for my buddy to sell the car, I was one of the first to test-drive it, and it was everything that I had dreamed. However, the price was out of my ballpark. I was so sad that I was just sick. My dream quickly faded to resignation. "I will never be able to buy that car," I sighed. Yet, I would've done anything to be able to own that automobile. Then, suddenly, my dream (or nightmare) was resurrected. I got a call a couple of days later. The car was for sale again. A previous buyer had dropped out, and the price was lowered significantly. It could be mine if only I would act immediately, I was told. So I did. I took my dad up to see it. We started it up and noticed that it had a funny sound but "not to worry, I'm sure it just needed oil or something." I told (or sold) my dad, who was anything but a mechanic. So I bought the car against his better judgment and became the proud owner of a broken car. It seems the previous owner used to run it pretty hard and burned out the bearings from over-revving the engine while street racing. The crankshaft was ruined, and it was getting ready to throw a tie rod. And I was too embarrassed to admit my ignorance and plead for my money to be returned. So instead of driving my car triumphantly the summer of my sixteenth year, I spent that entire summer rebuilding the engine.

And I mean completely. We tore that engine all the way down, got a new crankshaft, new bearings, new rods, new pistons and new rings, resurfaced the heads, got new gaskets, you name it. It took all summer to do, and on my budget it meant I worked during the day at a paying job and on that car at night and on the weekends. We (my twelve-year-old brother and I) somehow put it back together. Then we got it running again, and I drove it for a few months and then sold it for about what I'd originally paid for it. That was probably one of the stupidest decisions I've ever made: buying something because I so desperately desired it rather than acknowledging my dad's wisdom, which counseled me to let it go.

However, I can say that I learned a lot, and God continues to use the lessons of that automobile to provide direction and warning to me today. In fact, more than once that practical experience has helped me relate to the men at the Earnhardt Racing Shop, in the weekly Bible study. Of course, what they do is infinitely more sophisticated than what I did that summer.

You too have probably made your share of crummy decisions. And like me, you've probably had the good fortune to make a few good choices and are enjoying the blessings as a result. Probably my best decision was marrying my wife, Brenda. Having dated enough girls to know what I wanted and having not found what I knew would be best, I was one discouraged single man. Then, in 1975, at the ripe old age of twenty-two, I met the woman of my dreams and wonderful soon-to-be bride. I was really committed to being single because I have a high degree of experience in being selfish and enjoying my selfishness. I knew marriage would cost me a lot of independence, and it has. But it's still been one of the best decisions of my life. Brenda's just right for me and remains a constant source of blessing and joy so many years later. That's the way good decisions are. The positive results from them have a tendency to perpetuate themselves in your life.

In this next section of Scripture we are given the privilege of watching our Lord make a major decision. And this one is critical because it will affect the perpetuity of his life's message to bring the world to salvation through the gospel. Christ's process is simple but not easy, yet its labor yields an inestimable harvest of blessing. And its principles provide an airtight method for successfully making key decisions. Luke writes:

> One of those days Jesus went out to a mountainside to pray, and spent the night praying to God. When morning came, he called his disciples to him and chose twelve of them, whom he also designated apostles: Simon (whom he named Peter), his brother Andrew, James, John, Philip, Bartholomew, Matthew, Thomas, James son of Alphaeus, Simon who was called the Zealot, Judas son of James, and Judas Iscariot, who became a traitor.
>
> He went down with them and stood on a level place. A large crowd of his disciples was there and a great number of people from all over Judea, from Jerusalem, and from the coast of Tyre and Sidon, who had come to hear him and to be healed of their diseases. Those troubled by evil spirits were cured, and the people all tried to touch him, because power was coming from him and healing them all. (6:12-19)

Provocation

Normally, critical decisions have a precipitating event. For example, whether to have surgery or not is probably due to the previous diagnosis of a problem. So it is here with Jesus. Just as we discussed in chapter seven, when you're caught mid-idea in a text, it's necessary to back up and read the preceding account in order to fully appreciate the context. We have to ask ourselves what's going on. What we find is a growing resentment to Jesus. In fact, there was so much resistance to his ministry that his life was in danger. Our Lord knew that he was going to die sooner or later—we all do—but his death would be the basis for our redemption. It was necessary, though it would be violent and painful and the result of rejection. Though Jesus was literally in control of the timing, his prescribed mission nevertheless necessitated that he die. And here we see the timer go off toward the countdown to his crucifixion. In light of that, the question arises: How can he, with such an abbreviated life, hope to achieve the evangelization of the world? That is, how will he go about extending an invitation to men and women to receive God's forgiveness through faith if he's not around? How could he complete his mission if he was dead? That was the critical, strategic question Christ was faced with at this juncture, and his decision carried the weight of the world's salvation with it. Robert Coleman helps us with the answer:

> Jesus devoted most of his remaining life on earth to these remaining disciples. He literally staked his whole ministry upon them. The world could be indifferent towards him and not defeat his strategy. . . . Had Jesus given encouragement to popular sentiment among the masses he easily could have had all the kingdoms of men at his feet. . . . But Jesus would not play to the galleries. . . . Why? Why did Jesus deliberately concentrate his life on comparatively so few people? The answer of this question focuses at once the real purpose for his plan for evangelism. Jesus was not trying to impress the crowd but to usher in a kingdom. This meant that he needed men who could lead the multitudes. What good would it have been for his ultimate objective to

arouse the masses to follow him if these people had no subsequent supervision, no instruction in the Way? . . . Hence, he concentrated himself upon those who were to be the beginning of his leadership. Though he did what he could to help the multitudes he had to devote himself primarily to a few men rather than the masses in order that the masses could at last be saved. This was the genius of the strategy.[1]

Jesus knew better than all that he needed a few good men. But who? Of the many that listened and fewer that followed, which ones could be counted on to learn and then employ the methods our Lord wanted replicated?

Process
The process our Lord employed toward that pivotal selection had actually been intentional on his part over all these many months. It was perhaps not so obvious to us, but nevertheless it lay just under the surface in each account of his ministry. It was present the day he spoke in his home synagogue when he was mocked and run out of town. Obviously those people wouldn't do. It was present in each successive visit with Andrew, Peter, James and John. They listened; they were willing to help and trust and try. They were added to his short list. It was present with every confrontation with the Pharisees. They argued and opposed; they could never be trusted to represent him after his death. It was also present in his lecturing and miracles among the multitudes. They listened because they were curious or because they were hungry[2] but not because they were committed. So off the list they went. So who? How would he know?

He knew because he asked, and God gave him direction. According to Luke's account we are told that after his lengthy period of analysis, fact-finding and testing he submitted the issue before God in prayer. And his prayer was not a two-minute quickie but a lengthy conversation of fervent petition that took him all night. I have no doubt that this prayer included a recapitulation of his decision-making list.

Have you ever prayed through such a list yourself? I'm sure when you are in the midst of a major decision that you take time to list the pros and cons and the options available. You probably list the risks and the rewards. I think any good list would include, first, all the necessary information pertaining to the issue. Perhaps it would also include examples from your own experience of similar situations. It should include a review of Scripture that's relevant to the issue at hand, as well as the thoughts and counsel of trustworthy Christian friends. And then, finally and thoroughly, prayer—prayer throughout the process and prayer at the end.

I hope we see the value of prayer. I hope we do more than pay passing attention to the need to pray in decision-making. It doesn't have to take you all night (though it could), but it should be long enough to fully lay the matter before God and arrive at a sense of conviction at what it is that you should do. Afterward, if you're still not convinced, perhaps it's time to do nothing but gather more facts and wait for a better time while continuing to pray through until you have the confidence of God's direction.

Product

Well, the day of the decision has arrived, and it's time to pull the trigger. Hesitation will only cost you and those who rely on you. Jesus made his decision in prayer at night alone with God. But as soon as it was possible, the next morning he activated the decision in his selection. It was a specific and irreversible decision. And because it was pursued so purposely, it was an immeasurable success. In today's world all who know Christ personally can point to this decision as a reason the Christian sect didn't disappear into oblivion a few generations after the death of the founder. He selected well. He appointed men who would represent him faithfully and carry his life message and mission to the masses. And he selected well because he waited until the time was right and he had all the facts necessary to insure success.

But timing is key. If speed is not essential, timing is. And Christ made his decision right on time. He gave himself just enough time to train his men expertly before he launched them into the gospel ministry on their own.

Publicize

But Christ wasn't done with the decision-making process. No decision is complete until we inform all those who are affected. In this example he descended with the Twelve in order to announce his selection to the multitudes. This was subsequent to inviting them to a private conference where he conferred on them their new designation as his twelve apostles.[3] The men needed the assurance of knowing Christ himself had selected them. They didn't hear it secondhand. And the multitudes needed to be informed of the selection of these twelve delegates, for they would now begin to represent Christ to the people. Like interns, they would begin to perform many of his ministry duties as understudies and look back at this confirming moment in order to gain credibility before the masses and confidence in themselves.

Perseverance

Finally, I notice that it's business as usual. This decision didn't necessitate a huge change in operations. Christ went immediately back to his previous work. He kept on teaching, healing and helping those who were demonically oppressed. Good decisions do that. They extend your influence without altering your style. I can think of at least two significant outcomes of good or right decisions.

1. Good decisions are distinctive. They stand out from the rest of the decisions made in your life because of timeliness, impact or change. They are the high-water marks in a life of responsibility and authority that God has entrusted to you. I'm convinced that God doesn't expect us to be perfect in the decision-making process but to learn and improve. Otherwise he wouldn't have written Joel 2:25 and Isaiah 43:18. However, he does endow us with the capabilities we need as we trust him and appeal to his wisdom to do the right thing at the right moment when critical issues are on the line. And when we do, we'll notice that those good decisions stand above the rest. They mark the path of our life by their significance. Some of the marks include education, career, marriage, family and geographic location.

I remember my decision to marry Brenda. I had been thinking through the characteristics I most desired in a wife. I evaluated what I had to offer as well as my liabilities. I had dated extensively, testing other relationships for their compatibility, trying to discover what worked and what didn't, looking for that right chemistry. But when I proposed, it came spontaneously. I didn't plan on it—I just blurted it out one night as we shared an evening together. Was it a good decision? It was a great one! My life is so much fuller, happier and more effective than it would've been without her. Was it made too quickly? No. The process had been going on for years. Was it made prayerfully? Yes. Though I was not strong in my faith at that time, I did exercise the faith that I had to ask God to lead me to my wife. And has it set the course of my life? Yes, it has. If I had married another, who knows the direction I would've taken?

2. Good decisions act as our ambassadors. They extend our influence and our impact in our world of responsibility. And they reflect our character, values and faith. Looking back, I know that. I can see that my bad decisions limited my impact and truncated my opportunities. But when I do decide right, I notice that I grow and my influence grows and my impact is more strongly felt for Christ. My marriage, for example, has extended my influence to families and communities I had never dreamed of. It was also a reflection of my inner character. You can always tell that by the quality of the choice you've made.

Decision-making has essentially represented those two things throughout my life. I can see distinction and extensions in my college and career decisions, in decisions about children, lifestyle and other things. It's that way for you too.

So what's the downside? Bad decisions harm our influence and decrease our effectiveness. Bad decisions increase our stress and alter our relationships. Can we avoid them? Not all. But I do believe our decision-making batting average can improve as we follow the Master's plan for making life's choices. As a man, sincere, alert, seeking to follow the Master, I'm committed to processing decisions his way. Hold me to it, men. Let's do this together.

10

INTEGRITY

Implementing Your Ethic

LUKE 6:20-38

*O*ver lunch six of us were listening to two men describe the challenges they faced trying to maintain relationships with old friends who seemed bent on testing their faith. Bob, the first to speak, told story after story of trying circumstances where his buddy tried to push the moral envelope with him. Bob could have broken off the friendship with the man, but he desperately wanted to see his old school buddy come to faith in Christ. The friend, however, remained skeptical, "just waiting for me to goof up," Bob sighed, "so he could label me just another hypocritical Christian."

Then the conversation got really interesting. Bob, a successful investment broker, told us that recently another friend asked him a watershed question: "What would you do if your best client flew into town and wanted you to take him to a gentlemen's club?" Now, you need to understand the context of this question. Bob's clients are very successful people from all over the country and overseas. I thought I'd hear the typical businessmen's hedge. But instead Bob told us, with the matter-of-fact confidence of a man who had already thought this issue through and prepared his response, "Well, he wouldn't be my best client anymore. I would tell him that he'd have to go by himself." With that comment Gary, the other man at the table along with our three wives, then told us how he too had set boundaries for himself in order to maintain his testimony for Christ. I was fascinated as I listened to these two businessmen talk about the necessity for moral constraints as a visible demonstration of their Christian faith. They felt (and, of course, I agree) that being a Christian demands some drawing of lines (boundaries). They affirmed one another that they needed to develop a sense of what is and isn't permissible for them as Christian businessmen.

I was amazed. I've heard so much compromise through the years, so much justification, that I was delighted to see these two successful men have such a well thought-out sense of personal ethics. Understand, these men aren't rigid right-wing fundamentalists. In that discussion the question of a Cuban cigar and a glass of port was raised as an occasional pleasure they might enjoy from time to time. They wondered aloud as to the liberty of this against the effect of their testimony to other Christians, family, friends and business associates.

I enjoyed the time thoroughly as I listened to two good men of influence work through the very real options they face behaviorally as they acknowledged the need to establish self-imposed boundaries and not just back out of relationships. They do this both in recognition of their relationship to God and as a means of representing him to the world that they're privileged to be connected to. Their target ministry is their world of lost friends who all are searching for something and don't know where to go to find it.

I love that kind of personal transparency and community compassion. My lone contribution to the discussion was to agree with them that Christian men need to know what their boundaries will be and why they establish them, that the boundaries need to be their own and not borrowed from someone else.

For sake of discussion, let's look at these two points in reverse. Why set boundaries? What should they be?

Why Set Boundaries?

I think it's reasonable to say that the world is awash in moral relativism. "When 33 percent of married people cheat on their spouses, 90 percent of us lie regularly,"[1] 25 percent would abandon our families, and 7 percent would murder a stranger for 10 million dollars, according to one poll,[2] it is safe to wonder what moral or ethical fiber there is that will hold us together. If only 13 percent of Americans still believe in the moral authority of the Ten Commandments, what moral code will we abide by?

Ken Boa, in a fine article titled "What Is Behind Morality," informs us:

> No matter what their culture, people have moral experiences, aesthetic experiences, and religious experiences. The idea of right versus wrong and good versus bad is firmly entrenched in the human mind, and it is consistently displayed in the human experience. The norms of morality may vary, but all people tend to believe that some things are right and some things are wrong.
> . . . In India it is called the dharma or the rita. In China it is called the tao. In Christianity it is the Golden Rule, as set forth by

Christ. And the Silver Rule of Confucius is yet another. . . . Each person entertains the concept that some things are objectively right and other things are simply wrong.[3]

Ken is certainly right about the comprehensive nature of conscience and the intrinsic sense we all have of a code of right and wrong. Indeed, every culture and people have some behavioral sets of standards elevated as the moral target for their people.[4]

Despite the fact that all of the world's cultures have a moral code, humankind still suffers from every form of misconduct imaginable, with no relief in sight. Only Christianity proposes to change people's external behavior by first changing the heart, that is, our internal moral compass. Some can argue that several of the world's most heinous abuses of civil rights and moral impropriety have been perpetrated by Christians. But to know Christianity we must first know its founder, Jesus Christ, and what he represented. We must judge the philosophy by what he said and what he did, not by his imperfect followers.

Jesus never hurt anyone. His ethical prescriptions were the superlative of every human expectation. He was different. Jesus realized that moral compulsion would never make a person perfect or a society free from conflict. He realized that men and women would need a new nature in order to live nobly. Only with a changed heart will we have the ability to deny or suppress our base desires and selfishness. He also was aware that behavior based on the execution of goodness by others would never happen. Responding to others based on how they treat us would always degenerate into spite and retaliation. Why? Because others will fail us every time. Our natural tendency is to keep records on the behavior of our fellow humans and then to respond in kind. "You cut me off on the freeway, and I'll cut you off," and so forth.

Jesus revolutionized the way humankind is to treat one another when he said to "do to others what you would have them do to you" (Matthew 7:12). This golden rule of ethics put the responsibility of a better society on us, the listeners, instead of on our neighbors.

Christ's Golden Rule was a logical extension of his view of the law. He knew that the law was meant to ensure the health and welfare of humankind—not just for protection or justice. His summation of what was right and legally incumbent on humankind to perform was "love the Lord your God with all your heart and with all your soul and with all your mind" and "love your neighbor as yourself" (Matthew 22:37, 39). And with that he swept away the concept of justified retaliation as well as the notion of waiting to be done right before I do right to others.

Christians are enjoined to initiate the process of a moral, civil interchange between others and ourselves in the human race. I should add that Christ demonstrated this radical view of ethics in the sacrifice of his life for human sin. He substituted himself for all of us individual sinners. So he certainly has the right to challenge our preconceived notions of justice and authority. He also has the authority to call us to copy his lifestyle of self-denunciation and the forfeit of personal rights if it will help secure the welfare of our neighbors.

Jesus Christ did not let us off the hook with the caveat that our initiation or response to people is predicated on their worthiness. No, in fact, in the passage we are about to study, he dramatically declares his expectation that we are to respond nobly to those who have been ugly to us. This is revolutionary thinking. Yet it is right and yields a profound relational stability as well as providing us with peace and joy when implemented.

Let's see how he explains the issue of ethics in his famous Sermon on the Mount:

Looking at his disciples, he said:

"Blessed are you who are poor,
　for yours is the kingdom of God.
Blessed are you who hunger now,
　for you will be satisfied.
Blessed are you who weep now,
　for you will laugh.
Blessed are you when men hate you,
　when they exclude you and insult you
　and reject your name as evil,
　　because of the Son of Man.

"Rejoice in that day and leap for joy, because great is your reward in heaven. For that is how their fathers treated the prophets.

"But woe to you who are rich,
　for you have already received your comfort.
Woe to you who are well fed now,
　for you will go hungry.
Woe to you who laugh now
　for you will mourn and weep.
Woe to you when all men speak well of you,
　for that is how their fathers treated the false prophets.

"But I tell you who hear me: Love your enemies, do good to those who hate you, bless those who curse you, pray for those who mistreat you. If someone strikes you on one cheek, turn to him the other also. If someone takes your cloak, do not stop him from taking your tunic. Give to everyone who asks you, and if anyone takes what belongs to you, do not demand it back. Do to others as you would have them do to you.

"If you love those who love you, what credit is that to you? Even 'sinners' love those who love them. And if you do good to those who are good to you, what credit is that to you? Even 'sinners' do that. And if you lend to those from whom you expect repayment, what credit is that to you? Even 'sinners' lend to 'sinners,' expecting to be repaid in full. But love your enemies, do good to them, and lend to them without expecting to get anything back. Then your reward will be great, and you will be sons of the Most High, because he is kind to the ungrateful and wicked. Be merciful, just as your Father is merciful.

"Do not judge, and you will not be judged. Do not condemn, and you will not be condemned. Forgive, and you will be forgiven. Give, and it will be given to you. A good measure, pressed down, shaken together and running over, will be poured into your lap. For with the measure you use, it will be measured to you." (Luke 6:20-38)

Remember the context: he is in the midst of declaring to his men the moral expectation of those who represent him and seek to invite others to become members of Christ's kingdom. Therefore, he commands his men to consider values contrary to those of this temporal world. No one wants to be poor, hungry, sorrowful and hated, but compared to forgoing membership in Christ's eternal kingdom, these temporal hazards are a mere inconvenience.

If we can step back from life long enough to consider the breadth of our existence, we might assign a lower weight to today's troubles. It's like a painful savings program as we prepare for a future benefit. I might prefer the delight of self-indulgence today, but if I could save a little each month for a year or so, I will enjoy the incredible delight of a new toy, a nice vacation or resort home, etc. Most of us want our pleasure now, not later. But when you enter into a relationship with Christ, you are guaranteed a glorious future and equipped to represent his values now, even if it pains you. That's why I was so delighted in my two friends, Gary and Bob. They understood that truth and designed specific perimeters for themselves to operate within so that they could exemplify that principle. They are two true men of Christ. They now serve a spiritual kingdom instead of merely a physical one. They understand that they operate in both realms at one time, and when push comes to shove, they seek to choose what would please Christ over what would temporally provide for their comfort or personal goals. They understand the need to base moral decisions on a fixed absolute of right and wrong.

What Should the Boundaries Be?
And what is that absolute? From what basis did Gary and Bob develop their personal do and don't list? From Christ. Except Christ never publicized a do and don't list. Instead, he publicized an all-encompassing principle called the Golden Rule. It is a rule based on selflessness, a rule that is based on love.[5] This is the first ethical necessity of a Master's man.

This Golden Rule of ethics, which governs human relationships, is based on recognition of self-interest. It was the distillation of a comment Christ once made to a lawyer who wanted to know what Christ thought was the most important law of Judaism. Jesus' answer was simple but difficult: we were to love God with all our heart and others as ourselves. Jesus presented love as the foundation of the ethical system of Christianity. It is the basis of the eternal kingdom's moral code. That was revolutionary. It not only took away the burden of trying to remember and keep countless laws, it also guaranteed success by turning people's attention from failure, what they shouldn't do, to success—what they should do.

But how would it work in common, everyday experience? It would be hard and occasionally costly, but it would provide for a guiltless conscience, de-escalate tensions between people and cultivate goodwill between men.

In this sermon Christ outlined three virtues that are imperative for a Master's man to display. These are proof of our heavenly oriented ethical commitment. He said we should love, extend mercy and be generous. When we elevate love over hate, we give what's best for others, even our opponents. When we do that, we stop the growth of retaliation, remove any justification for harming us and develop true concern for the condition of the offender. This is the only way to bridge broken relationships and pursue reconciliation. It's not easy, but neither are constant conflict, lawsuits, divorce, fistfights and war.

We pray for world peace, but we won't step across the street to help an enemy in need. The emblem on the side of a police car that says peace officer is a joke. True peace will never be established by a badge, a gun or handcuffs. Peace is made possible by someone laying down arms and offering an extended hand of friendship. It may not always work, and it may be impossible at times, but it is the way of Christ's kingdom, and it does exemplify the moral values of the kingdom of heaven.

So the Master enjoins his men to pursue this track as the best alternative to society's way. And Christ reminds us that this type of self-sacrificing love is most effective when it is most unexpected. We exemplify Christ and his kingdom when we care for those who hurt and won't repay us, not when we serve our friends because that is expected.

Second, a Master's man extends mercy. Mercy normally elicits a sigh of relief and engenders appreciation from the recipient. But it is difficult to do. We are living in society where everyone demands their rights and wants full compensation for the wrongs they've received. It's hard to let go of a legitimate opportunity to be recompensed when we have it coming. But it not only pays great dividends to us and to them when we extend mercy, it also exemplifies the way Christ dealt with us. Christ forgave us and forgot our screwups (sin) when we deserved his wrath and punishment.

One day my son and I miscalculated the descent of a tree we were cutting down in the forest. It crushed my neighbor's back fence in spectacular style. After we got over the thrill of watching the tree fall and the fence explode in a hundred pieces, I marched to the neighbor's front door to give him the news. "Hi, I'm Jim Coté, one of your neighbors. I owe you some money." First he stuck out his hand, and then he yanked it back. "What's wrong?" he asked, bewildered. I shared what I had done, and we walked to the backyard to assess the damage. I apologized eyeball to eyeball with him and then offered to pay for the repair. He was a building contractor, and I used to be one, so we agreed I could fix it. Then his wife came out! Over and over she reminded me that this was *her* house. OK, I got it. Then she repeated how she didn't appreciate this incident that hurt her property, and she demanded reparation. She didn't get it that I got it, I guess.

Finally, after several apologies, I said, "That's why I came over immediately, to apologize, ma'am, and to make amends. However you want it handled, I'll be willing to do whatever it takes to make sure you're satisfied." Then I left her after reaffirming my intent with her husband. One hour later, thankfully, the fence was easily fixed. It was actually no big deal. But people are really uptight these days about their property and rights.

And woe unto you if you infringe on them.

That's why showing mercy is so unusual, so Christlike, so kingdom building and so effective in building bridges with people.

Finally, the Master said that his men are to be generous. They're givers not takers, and giving takes faith. Most of us work hard to make ends meet and to accumulate for our families. That's why relinquishing it seems absurd. Christ said there is a blessing in giving. We are freed from greed or from being owned by our property. Others are benefited, endearing them to us. And God compensates us, giving it all back and more.

Giving makes great sense when looked at this way. Recently a question arose as to how to counsel a Christian man who, having loaned thirty thousand dollars with interest to another Christian man, was not being paid back. The friend who brought the issue up had counseled his buddy to forget the loan, describing the transaction as a form of surety or cosigning, which Scripture warns us to resist.[6] I believe he's right, and I also believe that there are other biblical principles at stake such as honesty, debt responsibility, confrontation, restitution and church discipline, just to name a few. But I also have experienced the miracle of Luke 6:38 personally in my business experience. More than once when someone stole from me or didn't pay a bill in full, after exhausting all biblical and reasonable efforts to be repaid, I gave up the loss to God as an act of giving. And as I trusted him to provide my need, God always repaid me sometime later. Sometimes the repayment was incredible and in unexpected ways, but never has the Lord shorted me when I gave up something in the spirit of this verse. And certainly God has given to me in multiple ways for the free-will gifts and offerings to Christian people and causes as a biblical act of philanthropy.

As someone has well said, you can't outgive God. And this Scripture says as much. I believe it and have joyfully experienced it. Plus, this contrarian way of dealing with money exemplifies Christ. Another passage of Scripture tells us that giving generously and sacrificially promotes his kingdom and builds relationships.[7] To give like this means to provide for others as we relinquish ownership, understanding that God really owns all, and he repays generously to those that trust him.

So how should we live as Christians? What boundaries should we set ethically so we might exemplify Christ? It's as easy and difficult as showing love when we want to lash back, extending mercy when we could condemn, and giving generously when we would rather withhold. In other words, if in every situation we should ask ourselves what is the loving, merciful and generous thing to do in light of the fact that we serve a powerful king and a spiritual kingdom, the individual choices will be obvious.

Is there a do and don't list? No, there's not. It's not circumstantial or relative either. It's based on the absolute truth that we are to love God with all of our heart, soul, mind and strength, and to love others as ourselves. And in light of those two great principles we have the moral motivation to seek the most loving, merciful and generous thing to do at a given moment on behalf of our fellow human beings. When we seek to love like the Master loved, the to dos will naturally flow from that intent.

The result? I am convinced you will actually have more friends, sleep better at night and one day enjoy a great reward. I am trusting Christ to keep his word on this subject because I know he is a person of integrity.

11

COMMITMENT

Taking Responsibility for Yourself

LUKE 6:39-49

*C*ommitment. How do you define it? The *New World Dictionary* defines it as "a promise to do something, to set apart, to put to some purpose."[1] It is yet another value that's up for grabs in our world today.

Think about it. What is worthy of your pledge, promise or ultimate efforts? What are you totally set apart to accomplish?

I once read an amusing article in *USA Today* concerning the coach for the Oakland Raiders of the NFL. Every few years the sports page highlights a new hero of workaholism that supposedly sets the man apart from his peers as someone to admire because of the hours he works attempting to succeed. Jon Gruden, a young, bright, computer-adept head coach, is extolled for his 4:00 a.m. to 11:00 p.m. work hours during the football season. Gruden says he has too much to do to sleep. But Cindy, his wife, calls them "wacko" hours. She may be more on target than she imagines, or she may even be offering a subtle marital hint. Who knows? But the point is that Coach Gruden is displaying one form of commitment. The man has "set aside" a part of his life (sleeping) in order to "set apart" coaching football as his one encompassing purpose. It isn't that I don't admire his effort and endurance, but I do question the target.

I suppose everybody's committed to something. On one extreme there are those committed to rank laziness in the challenge to see if they can get by in life with the smallest possible contribution to their own well-being. Others, like those I recently read about in BUDS training (Basic Underwater Demolition-Seal), have an incredible commitment to endure physical punishment in order to survive a grueling test of teamwork, personal perseverance and raw courage to become a member of one of the most elite military units in the world. I wish I were that tough.

On the other end of the spectrum is former President Jimmy Carter who, at seventy-five, is still going full throttle in trying to represent his beliefs in practical avenues of humanitarian service. His work with Habitat for Humanity is well known. But I didn't realize that he's also involved in humanitarian efforts worldwide, including current projects in over sixty other nations. Here's a man who could be spending his days on the golf course or sipping mint julep with his lovely wife, Rosalynn, somewhere in Georgia on the porch of a plantation home. But he's committed to a different set of values: using the breadth of his life toward something that will endure beyond him. I admire that.

But it's still worth asking and answering the question—what exactly should we be committed to?

In the final section of Luke's Gospel that we shall look at

(Luke 6:39-49), we are challenged with the highest standard of conduct possible by our Master, the Lord Jesus Christ. In fact, it is infinitely higher than most of our society is accustomed to because his values emanate from the highest realm—heaven.

In this section (his famous Sermon on the Mount) Jesus calls those of us who are seeking to follow him to adopt his heavenly standards and express them in our daily conduct. So I think it's safe to say that the commitment Christ is calling us to is a commitment to him as a person. It might be illustrated by the ideals of marriage. When you're committed to a person, you can't help reflecting their values and adopting their perspective. You can't help caring deeply about what they care about. I realize in human relationships that there's compromise, resignation and even conflict. But in the perfect relationship that we're being offered from heaven, to have an intimate, vibrant experience with the living God, we are given a unique invitation to seek the best. The only compromise available is when we decide to live below God's standard, and the only conflict we will confront is when we reject the opportunity all together.

This passage clearly reveals that any commitment that marginalizes the invitation to imitate Christ is a commitment doomed to end in disappointment, even disaster. Certainly in this world someone's valiant efforts toward personal goals is worthy of some applause, even if it's only that we admire the person's grit. But ultimately the best applause will be reserved for those who not only strive valiantly but strive on the basis of a sure foundation that will secure a lasting reward. Let's see how Christ unwraps the package of that truth:

> He also told them this parable: "Can a blind man lead a blind man? Will they not both fall into a pit? A student is not above his teacher, but everyone who is fully trained will be like his teacher.

"Why do you look at the speck of sawdust in your brother's eye and pay no attention to the plank in your own eye? How can you say to your brother, 'Brother, let me take the speck out of your eye,' when you yourself fail to see the plank in your own eye? You hypocrite, first take the plank out of your eye, and then you will see clearly to remove the speck from your brother's eye.

"No good tree bears bad fruit, nor does a bad tree bear good fruit. Each tree is recognized by its own fruit. People do not pick figs from thornbushes, or grapes from briers. The good man brings good things out of the good stored up in his heart, and the evil man brings evil things out of the evil stored up in his heart. For out of the overflow of his heart his mouth speaks.

"Why do you call me, 'Lord, Lord,' and do not do what I say? I will show you what he is like who comes to me and hears my words and puts them into practice. He is like a man building a house, who dug down deep and laid the foundation on rock. When a flood came, the torrent struck that house but could not shake it, because it was well built. But the one who hears my words and does not put them into practice is like a man who built a house on the ground without a foundation. The moment the torrent struck that house, it collapsed and its destruction was complete." (Luke 6:39-49)

If you'll recall, when we studied the first section of Jesus' Sermon on the Mount (Luke 6:20-38), we saw that his ethical system demanded a new expectation in us. We are now to have an orientation that elevates the spiritual over the physical. This means we must recognize that God is the center of existence—we aren't. This perspective will force us to change the calibration of our ethical compass so that we initiate a new experience where we value love over hate and express that love in giving to others what's best for them, not withholding because of our selfish insecurity. We'll also show mercy instead of retaining our right to retaliate.

And now, by way of a parable, Christ brings these two great

philosophical principles down to two very important personal applications. In this last series of comments from his sermon he says that a Master's man has a choice to make. It is time to decide on our commitment. And to do that, he suggests that we walk through the following steps.

Evaluate

First a Master's man must evaluate his life. We must ruthlessly scrutinize our direction as well as the results based on the recognition of absolutes. You can't just follow any old philosophy, because if it goes into a ditch, you will too.

Years ago I was helped with this issue by going through some of Francis Schaeffer's work. I remember reading some of the condensed thoughts of Georg Wilhelm Friedrich Hegel (1770-1831). Hegel developed an interesting model that showed how cultures develop an evolving moral code in the absence of a commitment to absolutes. He summarized that the acceptable behavior of any particular era could be called the *thesis*. Normative behavior is always challenged by those seeking justification to step outside of societal norms and be accepted by the rest of society. So, as normative moral behavior is challenged by those wishing to liberate themselves from its confines, an extreme consideration of alternatives will emerge—to test the tolerance or acceptance of society. We'll call that extreme the *antithesis*. The antithesis of a current moral code is normally repugnant to any group of people, so a compromise takes place through the give-and-take of social debate that results typically in a new standard of acceptable behavior somewhere in the middle of the two extremes. This middle ground of compromise between competing ethical philosophies Hegel called a *synthesis*. Through this dynamic process of debate and experimentation a new moral code emerges that is now accepted by a broad representation of the populace. But the issue of acceptable behavior is not finished. Because of the dynamic nature of the process of redefining acceptable morality without the basis of an absolute standard, what occurs now is the natural degeneration of morals as the spectrum of what is acceptable in a culture moves gradually closer to the antithesis and away from the original starting point or thesis.

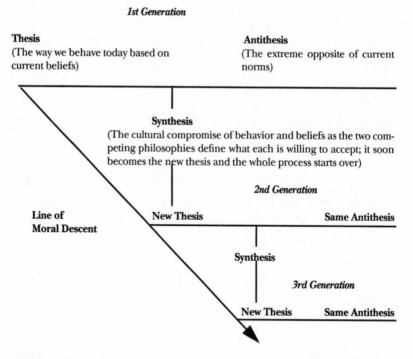

1st Generation

Thesis
(The way we behave today based on current beliefs)

Antithesis
(The extreme opposite of current norms)

Synthesis
(The cultural compromise of behavior and beliefs as the two competing philosophies define what each is willing to accept; it soon becomes the new thesis and the whole process starts over)

2nd Generation

Line of Moral Descent

New Thesis

Same Antithesis

Synthesis

3rd Generation

New Thesis

Same Antithesis

(By now we see a pattern as moral compromise leads society inevitably away from the old norms, gradually leading to new norms ever closer to what was once thought repugnant)

Figure 11.1. The evolution of moral degeneration

Amazingly, a culture that has adopted this new behavioral standard now defines the new behavioral allowances as the norm or thesis. And the process starts all over again. It doesn't take long for a society to accept as normative a standard of behavior that several generations ago would have been inconceivable—all because there is no fixed point from which to judge the legitimacy of behavior. And a culture that allows an evolution of its moral code after rejecting the orientation of a fixed standard of absolutes will always find itself adopting that which was once repugnant.

Perhaps I can illustrate this moral slide by using strip joints as an example. Thirty years ago American society viewed nudity as risqué and immoral. I remember a topless bar several miles down the road from our house in a run-down part of our city. When I turned twenty-one, the legal drinking age in California back then, I sneaked into the joint. I sneaked in not because it was illegal, but because it was viewed as immoral, and I didn't want anyone who knew me to see me enter. And what did I see? Actually, I remember the dark surroundings and the seedy people more than the nudity. Frankly, the environment was such a turnoff that I didn't go back. But today? Today we entertain clients at topless bars in order to show them a good time. Not only can we get away with it, but it's acceptable, a common practice in the business community. Of course, we've taken the immoral label off of them, and today we call them gentleman's clubs. In one stroke we've redefined both the concept of a gentleman as well as what is morally acceptable in terms of men viewing or gawking at or lusting for some strange woman's exposed body. How did this occur? We simply redefined moral adult entertainment by taking the old standard and contrasting it with the worst possible extreme—like what is done in the Mexican border towns in their fully naked, sexually explicit bars. And we decided, since we can't go that far, that maybe a peek at a woman's breasts isn't so bad after all. And so it goes from there.

The same scenario has occurred in the abortion phenomenon in this country. Previously an unwanted pregnancy was a shameful thing and not spoken of by women publicly for fear that their mothering instincts would be called into question. Then we decided, after the *Roe v. Wade* decision, that a doctor could remove a fetus if the life of the mother was in danger. From there we now accept the removal of unborn but living humans all the way into the third trimester and even partial-birth abortions for no other reason than the "woman's right to choose."

Now the acceptance of abortion has led to the discussion of acceptance of other forms of killing (called "the right to terminate life") such as euthanasia and genocide, and who knows what will be next as we move closer to the repugnant extreme that holds the incredible view that life isn't sacred, and terminating life (murder) is acceptable for any reason the murderer may deem necessary at the moment. I know it seems incredible, even impossible, but men, you are watching it happen. And it will continue until someone puts a stop to the slippery moral slope by leading others in a migration back to absolutes.

That is also how we have redefined success, heroism, liberty, marriage, fathering, financial responsibility and so forth. Give the Master credit here for warning us to watch those we are following lest we perish with them. And thank him for reminding us to reconsider absolutes.

He therefore gives us an opportunity to make a decision to evaluate our ethics based on his absolute ethical standard so that we can truly succeed in life. This will take commitment over convenience, as we shall see. In fact, it is a commitment that is evidenced by staying power through trial. People can say what they want about morals and ethical choices, but the fact is that what they do speaks louder than what they say. Look at the results of people's moral decisions, then decide for yourself. What do you want your life to look like when you reach the end? Your choice of ethical systems is critical. Depending on the one you choose, you may lose your way. So take time to reevaluate in order to avoid disaster.

Execute

Second, we are warned to execute—to follow through. Here we need to consider who we are listening to. Behavior is always the outgrowth of beliefs, and beliefs are developed initially by information. Who you listen to influences what you think, which influences what you believe to be true, which in turn influences what you do. Whose philosophy will you adopt? The universal law of pedagogy reveals that replication is the result of imitation. So who do you need to quit listening to? And with whom should you spend more time? Do you need to change any of your reading or viewing habits? Do you need to find a new radio station or form of entertainment? Just because there is freedom in our society and you have a lot of choices, that doesn't make every choice of equal benefit. Don't you think Satan has his propaganda machine in operation in America? I am not trying to be an alarmist, but there are plenty of wrong voices out there. Make sure you are tuned in to some of the more wholesome ones, and you'll be the benefactor; I guarantee it.

Furthermore, Christ discloses the fact that most of us aren't faithful to our own moral standards. We love to find fault with others. After all, that gives us a sense of superiority. But really, when we consider all the room for growth that we have, can we really afford the time to correct others verbally? And does telling our friends about others' failures really achieve anything anyway? Certainly we have something better to talk about than such hollow, self-aggrandizing drivel. We should concentrate on ourselves and not others.

So who can we follow? Whose standards are legitimate? We can begin to discover what's best by looking at the results of people's beliefs. Actions, as I've said, always emanate from beliefs, and beliefs from exposure to information, and so forth. So if you want to execute successfully, you must first consider the information you're fed and then look at its outcomes. For good can't come from bad and vice versa.

The best barometer of moral integrity is the heart. In the heart we settle on our deepest values, and we can't help but act these out in our daily experience. And, of course, to have the best heart we need to align our desires with those of Jesus, the author and perfecter of our faith. He initiated and fulfilled the philosophical system expressed in these verses. He did a perfect job of demonstrating these principles. Now he challenges us to follow in his footsteps, especially if we are going to call him Master. Whom will you follow? Will it be Jesus or someone else? Many say that they will, but they actually don't. Words, we know, are cheap; obedience is the final proof of faith. But allegiance to Christ brings security. Sure, Christ's way is difficult, challenging and countercultural, but it is also the only way to lasting contentment, joy and fulfillment. Those who think otherwise will surely live otherwise. And for a while they will even succeed. But in a world fraught with trouble, which guarantees all an ultimate appointment with death, you and I and everyone else are forewarned of a future time of proof-testing where the eternal impact of our choices will be revealed.

According to Luke 6:47-49 there is an impending test that will reveal the wisdom of the lifestyle we led, the strength of our commitment, and its inherent ability to stand secure under trial. Christ doesn't equivocate; he lays out the warning and the conclusion clearly. He says, "base your life on me and you will stand. Your life will be a success. You will remain after all else passes. But ignore me, choose an alternative lifestyle based on a competing conviction and, try as you may, you will fail. Your accumulation will be swept away and destroyed. Sorrow instead will be your destiny."

I'm so glad that I've been forewarned. Not everyone will tell you the risks associated with their product before you purchase. It took a court order to get warning labels on cigarettes—and then only after there were multiple product liability lawsuits due to the numerous cases of consumer dissatisfaction, disease and deaths. Those disastrous events finally resulted in consumer warnings on the package. But Christ doesn't operate that way. Satan has tried to keep his failed philosophy a secret, but Christ exposes the ineffective system with this parable. Jesus warns us of the risks associated with Satan's sandy system, and he is blunt about the consequences. He warns us clearly, concisely and conclusively. In fact, you might say the risk was all on him. Jesus risked his life with his words of encouragement, message of warning, and miracles that healed the sick while challenging the legitimacy and authority of the status quo leadership of his country. For his efforts, he was killed. But he won. He was right. His resurrection proved him right.

His testimony is that he is the Son of God, the spiritual is more significant than the physical, the eternal supersedes the temporal, and right overcomes wrong. He proved that love conquers hate, and giving eliminates greed. From him we learn that joy will overcome sorrow. He is worth all our faith, worthy of our obedience, and he will prove the truth of his words on the day of his coming. We can commit to him without fear or risk. Whatever cost we pay today to do so will be more than compensated by him later when we join him in his victorious resurrection called eternal life. He is Lord, and I am determined to follow and obey.

Amazingly, generation after generation seems to miss that simple yet essential fact. It is Jesus or nothing. Yes, I've tried to make that statement throughout this book, but let me say it now clearly and succinctly. If you follow Christ, you ultimately win. If you choose not to, you cannot win.

In 1998 thousands of Argentineans were swept away to a cruel death by floodwaters that raged through their residential community. Those houses they lived in were their homes. They were married there; they reared their children there. They worked there. It was their place of security. But, unfortunately, for over thirty thousand people, they had built their homes in the wrong place. The international community has been grieved by this horrific incident. Many of us have offered assistance toward the recovery of that area and its displaced people. But none of us can bring those lives back; none of us can turn back the clock to rectify the decision to build those homes in the wrong place. And, frankly, even if we could take a time machine back and walk through the streets of those hillside communities, I have to believe that next to no one would listen. It's amazing the momentum that is established by people following lost people. One person builds a home on the side of a steep ravine, not paying attention to the possibility of erosion produced by a heavy rainfall, and others soon follow. First, one family gets away with it for a few years, and then another family will build in the same location, and two will lead to three, and three to a dozen, and a dozen to a community. And then one fateful day, when the rains descend and the hillside becomes oversaturated, the ultimate truth that those homes were ill-built becomes self-evident. We might cheat physical law temporarily, but not ultimately. How much more true is the fact that we can't sidestep God's spiritual law. Jesus, the supreme Architect of the universe, the Creator of all that we see, the Savior of our own souls, has sounded a warning in this passage from Luke's Gospel. He calls us all to consider him in every aspect of life, not just believe on him for eternal life. He wants us to base our lives on him as the only true foundation for a successful life.

Will we heed him? As Master's men we have the opportunity to exceed the limits of the common life of our contemporaries. We have the privilege of knowing Christ intimately and following him not only into a glorious future but in the development of an effective life today.

He calls us to lift our vision above the mundane matters that tend to worry us to a grander vista of deep personal satisfaction, a panorama of beauty based on the reality that we can live successfully, securely, in step with him.

Summary

He will enable us to overcome temptation. He will give us a special purpose in life. He will graciously give us rest in the midst of our struggles. He will also make us a significant member of his team. The Master working through us will enable us to make an eternal difference in the lives of our neighbors. His imagination will stimulate us to develop effective new methods to address the needs of our ever-changing world. And his grace flowing through us will enable us to shed the scales of condemnation that have grown around us from a religious world that belittles those who know how to enjoy their freedom in Christ. Our Savior is *the* creator of the universe.[2] He designed us all, which enables him to give us the specific guidance we need in the midst of difficult decisions. He too can enable us to live ethically in a corrupt age. And he too allows us to become men of influence. But it all comes down to one thing: Will we commit to this glorious lifestyle?

I've always been impressed with the story of John Sculley's invitation to join Steve Jobs in the development of Apple Computer. Sculley had been the president of Pepsi Cola, and Jobs, the brilliant and relentless founder of Apple, had been courting Sculley for some time to join his team. Sculley's initial response to Jobs's proposal reminds me of so many men through the years who have come and gone through my life, men on the precipice of a life-changing decision, coming close to the edge but ultimately choosing the familiar over the adventure no matter how rewarding its potential may be.

Sculley's reply was, "I really love what you're doing at Apple, and I'm excited by it. How could anyone not be captivated, but it just doesn't make sense." Funny that this businessman was not even persuaded by the significant dollars offered (which was millions in compensation, signing bonus and severance)—what would it take to capture his imagination and ignite his commitment?

At last, Jobs, exasperated and frustrated, posed Sculley one last question, one that finally got his attention. He asked, "Do you want to spend the rest of your life selling sugar water or do you want a chance to change the world?"

Sculley writes, "It was as if someone reached up and delivered a stiff blow to my stomach. I had been worried about giving up my future at Pepsi, losing pensions and deferred compensation, violating the code of loyalty to Kendall, my ability to adjust in California—the pragmatic stuff that preoccupies the middle-aged. I was overly concerned with what would happen next week and the week after next. Steve was telling me my entire life was at a critical crossroads. The question was a monstrous one; one for which I had no answer. It simply knocked the wind out of me."[3] John Sculley's next breath included his decision to join Steve Jobs, and, as is often said, the rest is history.

Conclusion

Jesus offers the same kind of proposal to us and gives us the same freedom to accept or reject it. It's our choice. Christ's final offer in this parable is a monstrous one, and its significance is breathtaking. Do you want to do what you're doing today for the rest of your life for the same old reasons? Or do you want a chance to change the world? Are you willing to use what God's given you to do something significant for all the right but risky reasons? Or do you want to play it safe and achieve normal but temporary results?

The Master gives us all a chance to join him on an incredible journey where he will work through us to accomplish amazing things, but he won't force anyone. Each one of us must make an independent choice.

Unlike the Apple deal, we already know how his plan finishes. We just don't know yet the role he wants us to play in the drama. But we do know that it will be thrilling and life changing for us and those we influence. Are you ready to join him? Do you want to live by kingdom values or the world's? Do you want to be a Master's man or just a man? The choice is up to you.

Notes

Introduction
[1]Modern culture is quick to label anyone a hero, to the point where the word has all but lost its meaning. Successful athletes are heroes; honest politicians are heroes. People who return lost purses with the money still in them are heroes. As Florence King has observed, all anyone has to do to become a hero in America today is fall in a hole and live to tell about it.

But without absolutes there could be no heroes. "Real heroes are not now and were never defined by degrees of success; or by doing something they should do anyway even if most people don't; or, except in rare cases, by a single awe-inspiring moment of courage. Rather they are those people blessed and burdened with a God-given vision for improving their world that requires them to make a conscious, voluntary, life-changing sacrifice, which they make unhesitantly and without complaint" (John Perry, *Sgt. York: His Life, Legend & Legacy* [Nashville: Broadman & Holman, 1997], p. 331).

Chapter 1: Really Getting Started
[1]James Allan Francis, *The Real Jesus and Other Sermons* (Philadelphia: Judson Press, 1926), p. 123.

[2]"I tell you the truth, anyone who has faith in me will do what I have been doing. He will do even greater things than these, because I am going to the Father" (John 14:12). See also John 20:21-22 and 2 Corinthians 2:14; 3:5; 4:7; 5:17.

[3]"Then Jesus came from Galilee to the Jordan to be baptized by John. But John tried to deter him, saying, 'I need to be baptized by you, and do you come to me?' " (Matthew 3:13-14).

[4]"For all have sinned and fall short of the glory of God" (Romans 3:23).

[5]"Therefore, just as sin entered the world through one man, and death through sin, and in this way death came to all men, because all sinned—for before the law was given, sin was in the world. But sin is not taken into account when there is no law. Nevertheless, death reigned from the time of Adam to the time of Moses, even over those who did not sin by breaking a command, as did Adam, who was a pattern of the one to come" (Romans 5:12-14).

[6]"The LORD God took the man and put him in the Garden of Eden to work it

and take care of it. And the LORD God commanded the man, 'You are free to eat from any tree in the garden; but you must not eat from the tree of the knowledge of good and evil, for when you eat of it you will surely die' " (Genesis 2:15-17).

[7]"For the wages of sin is death, but the gift of God is eternal life in Christ Jesus our Lord" (Romans 6:23).

[8]"Regarding his Son, who as to his human nature was a descendant of David, and who through the Spirit of holiness was declared with power to be the Son of God by his resurrection from the dead: Jesus Christ our Lord" (Romans 1:3-4).

[9]"Peter replied, 'Repent and be baptized, every one of you, in the name of Jesus Christ for the forgiveness of your sins. And you will receive the gift of the Holy Spirit' " (Acts 2:38).

[10]"Praise be to the God and Father of our Lord Jesus Christ, who has blessed us in the heavenly realms with every spiritual blessing in Christ" (Ephesians 1:3).

[11]"All the prophets testify about him that everyone who believes in him receives forgiveness of sins through his name" (Acts 10:43).

"He then brought them out and asked, 'Sirs, what must I do to be saved?'

"They replied, 'Believe in the Lord Jesus, and you will be saved—you and your household' " (Acts 16:30-31).

"God made him who had no sin to be sin for us, so that in him we might become the righteousness of God" (2 Corinthians 5:21).

Chapter 2: Temptation

[1]"For we do not have a high priest who is unable to sympathize with our weaknesses, but we have one who has been tempted in every way, just as we are—yet was without sin" (Hebrews 4:15).

[2]Alfred Edersheim, *The Life and Times of Jesus the Messiah* (Grand Rapids, Mich.: Eerdmans, 1990), p. 292.

[3]"And I will ask the Father, and he will give you another Counselor to be with you forever—the Spirit of truth. The world cannot accept him, because it neither sees him nor knows him. But you know him, for he lives with you and will be in you" (John 14:16-17).

[4]"Whoever does not love does not know God, because God is love" (1 John 4:8).

[5]"Jesus answered, 'I am the way and the truth and the life. No one comes to the Father except through me' " (John 14:6).

[6]"You belong to your father, the devil, and you want to carry out your father's desire. He was a murderer from the beginning, not holding to the truth, for there is no truth in him. When he lies, he speaks his native language, for he is a liar and the father of lies" (John 8:44).

[7]"No temptation has seized you except what is common to man. And God is

faithful; he will not let you be tempted beyond what you can bear. But when you are tempted, he will also provide a way out so that you can stand up under it" (1 Corinthians 10:13).

[8]Bruce Wilkinson, *Personal Holiness in Times of Temptation* (Eugene, Ore.: Harvest House, 1998), p. 150.

[9]"By myself I can do nothing; I judge only as I hear, and my judgment is just, for I seek not to please myself but him who sent me" (John 5:30).

"For I have come down from heaven not to do my will but to do the will of him who sent me" (John 6:38).

[10]"But seek first his kingdom and his righteousness, and all these things will be given to you as well" (Matthew 6:33).

[11]The temple in Jerusalem went through various constructions and restorations, but at the time of Christ the temple was several stories high.

[12]"Fear the LORD your God, serve him only and take your oaths in his name" (Deuteronomy 6:13).

[13]"For he will command his angels concerning you
to guard you in all your ways" (Psalm 91:11).

[14]"Whether you turn to the right or to the left, your ears will hear a voice behind you, saying, 'This is the way; walk in it' " (Isaiah 30:21).

[15]"No temptation has seized you except what is common to man. And God is faithful; he will not let you be tempted beyond what you can bear. But when you are tempted, he will also provide a way out so that you can stand up under it" (1 Corinthians 10:13).

[16]"Jesus answered, 'It is written: "Man does not live on bread alone, but on every word that comes from the mouth of God" ' " (Matthew 4:4).

[17]Phillips Brooks, quoted in Stephen Covey, *The 7 Habits of Highly Effective People* (New York: Simon & Schuster, 1989), p. 297.

[18]On January 19, 1999, George Stephanopoulos watched as President Clinton gave his State of the Union address on the heels of the House's impeachment just days before. The president was confident, even cocky, as he gave his speech, yet a firestorm was brewing around him, and no one knew at that time where it would end. Stephanopoulos, no longer an adviser to the president, "watched from far away, enjoying the show but wondering too. Wondering what might have been—if only this good president had been a better man" (George Stephanopoulos, *All Too Human* [New York: Little Brown, 1999], p. 443).

Chapter 3: Mission

[1]"Profile of Nelson Rolihlahla Mandela" (February 2001), African National Congress <www.anc.org.za/people/mandela.html >.

[2]David Rockefeller, quoted in Fred Smith, *Learning to Lead* (Carol Stream, Ill.: Christianity Today Leadership/Word Book, 1986), p. 33.

[3]"And I will ask the Father, and he will give you another Counselor to be with

you forever—the Spirit of truth. The world cannot accept him, because it neither sees him nor knows him. But you know him, for he lives with you and will be in you" (John 14:16-17).

"But when he, the Spirit of truth, comes, he will guide you into all truth. He will not speak on his own; he will speak only what he hears, and he will tell you what is yet to come. He will bring glory to me by taking from what is mine and making it known to you" (John 16:13-14).

[4]Bob Shank, *Total Life Management* (Portland, Ore.: Multnomah Press, 1990), pp. 26-27, chap. 5.

[5]For more detailed information on this process, I recommend a helpful exercise in career assessment that will be professionally analyzed by the career assessment team at the Hendricks group: <Billh@hendricksgroup.com >.

Chapter 4: Solitude

[1]Tim Hansel, *When I Relax I Feel Guilty* (Elgin, Ill.: Cook, 1979), p. 22.

[2]Richard A. Swenson, *Margin* (Colorado Springs: NavPress, 1992), pp. 115, 228-29.

[3]Richard Flourney et al., *How to Beat Burnout* (Chicago: Moody Press, 1986), pp. 15, 105-6.

[4]"The LORD said, 'Go out and stand on the mountain in the presence of the LORD, for the LORD is about to pass by.'

"Then a great and powerful wind tore the mountains apart and shattered the rocks before the LORD, but the LORD was not in the wind. After the wind there was an earthquake, but the LORD was not in the earthquake. After the earthquake came a fire, but the LORD was not in the fire. And after the fire came a gentle whisper . . . [and] a voice said to him . . . and the LORD said to him" (1 Kings 19:11-15).

[5]"Very early in the morning, while it was still dark, Jesus got up, left the house and went off to a solitary place, where he prayed" (Mark 1:35).

Chapter 5: Team

[1]Robert Coleman, *The Master Plan of Evangelism* (Grand Rapids, Mich.: Baker, 1993), pp. 22-24, 27.

[2]Simon is also referred to in Scripture as Simon Peter or Peter.

[3]"Andrew, Simon Peter's brother, was one of the two who heard what John had said and who had followed Jesus. The first thing Andrew did was to find his brother Simon and tell him, 'We have found the Messiah' (that is, the Christ). And he brought him to Jesus" (John 1:40-42).

[4]"After John was put in prison, Jesus went into Galilee, proclaiming the good news of God. 'The time has come,' he said. 'The kingdom of God is near. Repent and believe the good news!'

"As Jesus walked beside the Sea of Galilee, he saw Simon and his brother Andrew casting a net into the lake, for they were fishermen" (Mark 1:14-16).

[5]See Psalm 75:6-7; 103:19; Daniel 4:17; Matthew 6:25-34.

[6]"I am the vine; you are the branches. If a man remains in me and I in him, he will bear much fruit; apart from me you can do nothing" (John 15:5).

[7]"But now a righteousness from God, apart from law, has been made known, to which the Law and the Prophets testify. This righteousness from God comes through faith in Jesus Christ to all who believe. There is no difference, for all have sinned and fall short of the glory of God, and are justified freely by his grace through the redemption that came by Christ Jesus" (Romans 3:21-24).

"Therefore, since we have been justified through faith, we have peace with God through our Lord Jesus Christ" (Romans 5:1).

[8]"And without faith it is impossible to please God, because anyone who comes to him must believe that he exists and that he rewards those who earnestly seek him" (Hebrews 11:6).

[9]"The rich rule over the poor,
     and the borrower is servant to the lender" (Proverbs 22:7).

"A generous man will himself be blessed,
     for he shares his food with the poor" (Proverbs 22:9).

[10]"Husbands, love your wives, just as Christ loved the church and gave himself up for her to make her holy, cleansing her by the washing with water through the word, and to present her to himself as a radiant church, without stain or wrinkle or any other blemish, but holy and blameless. In this same way, husbands ought to love their wives as their own bodies. He who loves his wife loves himself. After all, no one ever hated his own body, but he feeds and cares for it, just as Christ does the church" (Ephesians 5:25-29).

"Husbands, in the same way be considerate as you live with your wives, and treat them with respect as the weaker partner and as heirs with you of the gracious gift of life, so that nothing will hinder your prayers" (1 Peter 3:7).

[11]"Fathers, do not exasperate your children; instead, bring them up in the training and instruction of the Lord" (Ephesians 6:4).

[12]"Train a child in the way he should go,
     and when he is old he will not turn from it" (Proverbs 22:6).

[13]"The thief comes only to steal and kill and destroy; I have come that they may have life, and have it to the full" (John 10:10).

"Praise be to the God and Father of our Lord Jesus Christ, who has blessed us in the heavenly realms with every spiritual blessing in Christ" (Ephesians 1:3).

"Now to him who is able to do immeasurably more than all we ask or imagine, according to his power that is at work within us, to him be glory in the church and in Christ Jesus throughout all generations, for ever and ever! Amen" (Ephesians 3:20-21).

Chapter 6: Impact

[1] " 'The person with such an infectious disease must wear torn clothes, let his hair be unkempt, cover the lower part of his face and cry out, "Unclean! Unclean!" As long as he has the infection he remains unclean. He must live alone; he must live outside the camp' " (Leviticus 13:45-46).

[2]"Say to those with fearful hearts,
   'Be strong, do not fear;
  your God will come,
    he will come with vengeance;
with divine retribution
    he will come to save you.'
Then will the eyes of the blind be opened
    and the ears of the deaf unstopped.
Then will the lame leap like a deer,
    and the mute tongue shout for joy.
Water will gush forth in the wilderness
    and streams in the desert" (Isaiah 35:4-6).

"The Spirit of the Sovereign LORD is on me,
because the Lord has anointed me
to preach good news to the poor.
He has sent me to bind up the brokenhearted,
    to proclaim freedom for the captives
    and release from darkness for the prisoners,
to proclaim the year of the LORD'S favor
    and the day of vengeance of our God,
to comfort all who mourn,
    and provide for those who grieve in Zion—
to bestow on them a crown of beauty
    instead of ashes,
the oil of gladness
    instead of mourning,
and a garment of praise
    instead of a spirit of despair.
They will be called oaks of righteousness,
    a planting of the LORD
    for the display of his splendor.

They will rebuild the ancient ruins
    and restore the places long devastated;
they will renew the ruined cities
    that have been devastated for generations" (Isaiah 61:1-4).

Chapter 7: Change

[1]Jim Wright, quoted in Jane McAlister Pope, "Observations," *Charlotte Observer,* December n.d., 1999, sec. C, p. 4.

[2]H. Norman Wright, *Seasons of a Marriage* (Ventura, Calif.: Regal, 1982).

[3]Alfred Edersheim, *The Life and Times of Jesus the Messiah* (Grand Rapids, Mich.: Eerdmans, 1990), p. 129.

[4]"Therefore, if anyone is in Christ, he is a new creation; the old has gone, the new has come!" (2 Corinthians 5:17).

[5]"For all have sinned and fall short of the glory of God" (Romans 3:23).

[6]"So the law was put in charge to lead us to Christ that we might be justified by faith" (Galatians 3:24).

[7]"Abram believed the LORD, and he credited to him as righteousness" (Genesis 15:6).

[8]"We are therefore Christ's ambassadors, as though God were making his appeal through us. We implore you on Christ's behalf: Be reconciled to God" (2 Corinthians 5:20).

[9]Frank Tillapaugh, *Unleashing the Church* (Ventura, Calif.: Regal, 1982), p. 80.

[10]"Let us not give up meeting together, as some are in the habit of doing, but let us encourage one another—and all the more as you see the Day approaching" (Hebrews 10:25).

[11]Peter Drucker, *Innovation and Entrepreneurship* (New York: Harper & Row, 1985), p. 39.

Chapter 8: Rigidity

[1]"The LORD is compassionate and gracious,
   slow to anger, abounding in love" (Psalm 103:8).

[2]"He predestined us to adoption as sons through Jesus Christ to Himself, according to the kind intention of His will" (Ephesians 1:5 NASB).

[3]*New World Dictionary* (Cleveland: Williams Collins, 1979), p. 806.

[4]"What, then, was the purpose of the law? . . . Is the law, therefore, opposed to the promises of God? Absolutely not! For if a law had been given that could impart life, then righteousness would certainly have come by the law. But the Scripture declares that the whole world is a prisoner of sin, so that what was promised, being given through faith in Jesus Christ, might be given to those who believe.

"Before this faith came, we were held prisoners by the law, locked up until faith should be revealed. So the law was put in charge to lead us to Christ that we might be justified through faith. Now that faith has come, we are no longer under the supervision of the law.

"You are all sons of God through faith in Christ Jesus" (Galatians 3:19-26).

[5]Charles R. Swindoll, *The Grace Awakening* (Waco, Tex.: Word, 1996), p. xv.

[6]"By the seventh day God had finished the work he had been doing; so on the seventh day he rested from all his work" (Genesis 2:2).

[7]Merrill Unger, *Unger's Bible Dictionary* (Chicago: Moody Press, 1979), p. 940.

[8]Ibid.

[9]"So whatever you believe about these things keep between yourself and God. Blessed is the man who does not condemn himself by what he approves" (Romans 14:22).

[10]Read Romans 14 and 1 Corinthians 8 for further help.

[11]Alexander Solzhenitsyn, quoted in Max DePree, *Leadership Is an Art* (New York: Doubleday, 1989), p. 50.

[12]"To the Jews who had believed him, Jesus said, 'If you hold to my teaching, you are really my disciples. Then you will know the truth, and the truth will set you free' " (John 8:31-32).

[13]Thank God with me that Christ said in John 8:32 that "you will know the truth and the truth will set you free." And we know that Jesus Christ himself was "the way and the truth and the life" (John 14:6). Let's do what we can to introduce others to that life so they might enjoy the reprieve God intends for them. Christ was offering the kingdom through his message; he was modeling the kingdom through his lifestyle, elevating others in promoting joy and purity. He provided access to the kingdom through his death, and he will establish the kingdom when he returns. But many opposed him then by misunderstanding his intent, distorting his actions, maligning his character and seeking to intimidate his would-be followers. But we must separate the wheat from the chaff by asking ourselves what the character of God is like and if he is manifest in this approach or another. It is hard to imagine a good and gracious God represented by such sour and small-minded people who won't allow nourishment to the hungry or healing to the sick. And today so many are driven from an invitation to know God by the hard-boiled demands of legalists who say they represent him. It is more consonant with the character of God to see mercy on display. How winsome it is to find someone who won't hold our faults against us, who accepts us as we are, who helps us in our area of need without a laundry list of prerequisites. Love and grace and mercy are characteristics of God and are expected to be present in his followers. Jesus exemplified these and would court no dissenters, for these characteristics were critical to the mission of drawing men and women to salvation. We must do the same by making sure we are living by love, not retaliating against those who attack us or capitulating to their intimidation. We must examine our motives and, if affirmed, stay on track. We must proactively be seeking grace and doing what's best for others. In summary, we must rely on the grace of God.

Chapter 9: Decisions

[1]Robert Coleman, *The Master Plan of Evangelism* (Grand Rapids, Mich.: Baker, 1993), pp. 27, 29, 31, 33.

[2]"I tell you the truth, you are looking for me, not because you saw miraculous

signs but because you ate the loaves and had your fill" (John 6:26).

[3]The word *apostle* comes from the Greek *apostolos,* meaning "a person sent" or "one commissioned" (A. F. Walls, "Apostle," in *New Bible Dictionary,* ed. I. Howard Marshall, et al., 3rd ed. [Downers Grove, Ill.: InterVarsity Press, 1996], p. 58).

Chapter 10: Integrity

[1]Nimrod McNair, newsletter article from the Executive Leadership Foundation, Inc. (Atlanta, 1991).

[2]R. Kent Hughes, *Disciplines of a Godly Man* (Wheaton, Ill.: Crossway, 1991), p. 119.

[3]Ken Boa, "What Is Behind Morality," in *Living Ethically in the '90s,* ed. J. Kerby Anderson (Wheaton, Ill.: Victor, 1990), pp. 34-36.

[4]George Manning and Kent Curtis, *Ethics at Work* (Cincinnati: South-Western, 1989), pp. 64-71. Furthermore, I have found that the Communists have a code of ethics as well, called the Thirteen Points of a Secular Code of Ethics. Confucianism posits its quest for right relationships. Buddhists add their Four Noble Truths and their Noble Eightfold Path. Hinduism teaches Ten Great Virtues. Judaism presents the famous Mosaic code of Ten Commandments, and Islam seeks adherence to Three Conformities (its articles of faith, right conduct and religiosity) (John B. Noss, *Man's Religions* [New York: Macmillan, 1980], pp. 505-12).

[5]Agape love is defined as doing what is best for the other even it if dictates great cost to ourselves.

[6]"Do not be a man who strikes hands in pledge
    or puts up security for debts" (Proverbs 22:26).

[7]"For you know the grace of our Lord Jesus Christ, that though he was rich, yet for your sakes he became poor, so that you through his poverty might become rich" (2 Corinthians 8:9).

Chapter 11: Commitment

[1]*New World Dictionary* (Cleveland: Williams Collins, 1979), p. 286.

[2]"For by him all things were created; things in heaven and on earth, visible and invisible, whether thrones or powers or rulers or authorities; all things were created by him and for him" (Colossians 1:16).

[3]John Sculley and John A. Byrne, *Odyssey: Pepsi to Apple* (San Francisco: Harper & Row, 1984).